The Red Baron and Eddie Rickenbacker: The Lives and Legacies of World War I's Most Famous Aces

By Charles River Editors

A German postcard featuring the Red Baron

About Charles River Editors

Charles River Editors provides superior editing and original writing services across the digital publishing industry, with the expertise to create digital content for publishers across a vast range of subject matter. In addition to providing original digital content for third party publishers, we also republish civilization's greatest literary works, bringing them to new generations of readers via ebooks.

Sign up here to receive updates about free books as we publish them, and visit Our Kindle Author Page to browse today's free promotions and our most recently published Kindle titles.

Introduction

Manfred von Richthofen (1892-1918)

"Now I am within thirty yards of him. He must fall. The gun pours out its stream of lead. Then it jams. Then it reopens fire. That jam almost saved his life." – The Red Baron

Few participants in World War I are more famous than Manfred Albrecht Freiherr von Richthofen, better known as the Red Baron. A German known for victories in a war that his country lost, a cavalry officer made famous as mounted combat disappeared, and an aristocratic hero in a century dominated by democracy; Richthofen's celebrity stands in stark contrast to the era.

Furthermore, World War I is not remembered as a period in which the advance of technology empowered or emboldened individual human beings, and it certainly did not support the old romantic image of the lone, skilled warrior. The terrible grinding power of Europe's first great industrial war saw advances in gunnery and factory production that chewed up millions of young men and spit them out in fragments across the anonymous mud of no man's land. A soldier was more likely to be killed by an artillery shell flung from half a mile away than up close in combat, where his own skills might save his life, so there was little heroism and no glory to be found in the forms of violence provided by the modern war machine.

However, for the handful of men fighting in the air, it was a different matter, because World War I brought about the emergence of full-blooded aerial combat for the first time. In fact, airplanes were so foreign to past examples of warfare that few military officers were sure of how to utilize them at the start of the war. As a result, amazing new machines capable of carrying men at great speed and height were used first for reconnaissance, and it was only later that they actually became fighter planes, with each side fighting for dominance of the air and the advantage this provided. This was the era of the dogfight, in which aerial combat was effectively invented, with engineers and pilots working quickly to adapt machines and tactics to a whole new sort of warfare. In the skies above Europe, a man could once more play the role of the lone warrior, surviving or dying by skill and the power of personality.

Into this cloud-strewn battlefield came a young man from a young country, ready to prove not only his potential but that of the new form of combat at which he would excel. Indeed, there was no greater ace during the war than the Red Baron, who was credited with shooting down 80 Allied planes. However, the Red Baron's most remarkable accomplishment was one he never wanted. On April 21, 1918, while flying over the Somme, the Red Baron spotted an Allied plane and pursued it, and while in pursuit, the Red Baron was shot by a single bullet in the chest, mortally wounding him. Debate has raged ever since over whether an Allied pilot or infantry unit shot him, but either way, despite being mortally wounded and already near death, the Red Baron managed to land his plane in a field. He died almost immediately after the landing, and his plane quickly became a treasure trove for souvenirs among soldiers from the Allied Powers on the ground.

By the time he died at the age of 25, Richthofen was a living legend, celebrated by his fellow countrymen and feared by his enemies. Ironically, he had managed to become a celebrity soldier in an era of anonymous death.

Eddie Rickenbacker

"Courage is doing what you are afraid to do. There can be no courage unless you are scared."
– Eddie Rickenbacker

The men and women who won World War II for the Allies have been called "the greatest generation," and rightfully so, for they saved the Western world from destruction and domination by totalitarian dictators. As Winston Churchill so eloquently put it, "Never in the field of human conflict was so much owed by so many to so few." However, even within this glorious group, there was another, perhaps even more superlative generation made up of men and women who fought not only in World War II but also World War I, which at the time was the deadliest and most destructive war in history.

A few of these fighters were young enough to fight in both wars, and Eddie Rickenbacker was one of them, one of the "best of the best." Though he served only in a civilian capacity during World War II, he remains today a romantic hero of a bygone era, a man who flew airplanes that were little more than hang gliders with engines and guns, and survived to help design jets. His service won him the Medal of Honor, along with more awards for valor than any other person fighting in World War I.

But participating in the wars was not nearly enough time in the air for the ambitious Rickenbacker. When he was not setting new records in the air, he was setting new speed records on the ground, most notably as a first generation race car driver who not only drove cars but designed them. He also served for decades as the president of one of the world's first major commercial passenger aviation companies, Eastern Air Lines, seeing it through the ups and downs of the financial and technological boom and bust in America between the wars.

Richthofen's Early Years

"I never was good at learning things. I did just enough work to pass. In my opinion it would have been wrong to do more than was just sufficient, so I worked as little as possible." – Manfred von Richthofen

Understanding any great historical figure starts with understanding the world into which they were born, and in Manfred von Richthofen's case, that was the world of the German aristocracy. Though people had talked about Germany as a region for centuries, it was only united as a single country in 1871 under the ruthlessly effective leadership of Prussian Chancellor Otto von Bismarck. Bismarck united the disparate principalities of northern central Europe into a single German Empire under the Prussian monarchs, and it was an empire united by war, not through the conquest of other German nations by the Prussians but by bringing them together in the face of a series of external enemies, including Denmark, Austria and finally France. Shared military endeavour was therefore at the heart of German identity, especially for its aristocracy.

Though not long united politically, the whole German region shared a traditional aristocracy dating back to the Holy Roman Empire. The small German states had long been ruled by princes, lords and petty monarchs, now brought together in a single system. These aristocrats held a wide range of different titles, but they shared in the social, economic and political privilege common to aristocrats in all places and times, and with them a sense of superiority and entitlement.

At the top of the aristocratic chain was the Emperor or Kaiser, who from June 1888 was Wilhelm II, but his position, like that of the rest of the aristocracy, was an increasingly tenuous one. Their nation lacked the long-standing unity of Europe's other great powers, like Britain, France, Russia and the Austro-Hungarian Empire, and Germany also lacked the overseas colonies which gave status and economic power to many other countries, in particular Britain. Furthermore, the revolutions that had shaken 19th century Europe had seen monarchs and aristocrats overthrown, and Germany itself had been thrown into turmoil during the revolts of 1848. With that, a new power elite consisting of merchants and industrialists, men empowered by new technology and new money, was on the rise.

If the German elite felt insecure, then they compensated with a militaristic culture in which skill in hunting and warfare were highly prized. For the many minor aristocrats of the new German nation, there was no higher honor than to become an officer serving their country, preparing to fight the enemies that surrounded Germany on every front, and that would play a huge role in the life of the Red Baron.

Richthofen's coat of arms

Manfred von Richthofen was born in Silesia on May 2, 1892, and as a minor Prussian aristocrat, his upbringing included the hunting skills so popular among Europe's traditional upper class, with their warlike ancestors and their ownership of vast swathes of land. As such, he was destined from the start to join the army, and Manfred became an officer cadet at the age of 11. As he later pointed out, "As a little boy of eleven I entered the Cadet Corps. I was not particularly eager to become a Cadet, but my father wished it. So my wishes were not consulted."

In 1912, Manfred was commissioned into the cavalry, still a prestigious branch of the military, and one ideally suited to a young man of his aristocratic and sporting background. An officer in the 1st Regiment of Uhlans, a promising career fighting from horseback lay ahead of him. As he once said, "Of course no one thought of anything except of attacking the enemy. It lies in the instinct of every German to rush at the enemy wherever he meets him, particularly if he meets hostile cavalry." Later in the war, he would also say, "That was a beautiful time. We cavalry men who had already been in touch with the enemy and had seen something of war, were envied by the men of the other armies. For me it was the most beautiful time during the whole of the war. I would much like to pass again through the beginning of the war."

However, such fighting would soon be a thing of the past, as cavalry warfare became useless in the face of machine-guns and artillery bombardments. Thus, while no one could have predicted it in 1912, this young officer's future instead lay in the air. Although it's often forgotten today, the idea of turning the air into a theatre of war had been around since the late 18th century; the Montgolfier brothers' first manned hot air balloon flight in 1783 was followed in less than a year by the first pamphlet recommending the use of this new invention in warfare. However, it was not until the 1890s that manufacturing technology allowed the creation of the dirigibles which would turn military airpower into a reality. In the decade leading up to World War I, the nations of Europe were looking to the skies and considering how real, functional military airpower would look, and for Germany, the process of turning these considerations into a reality began when the Military Board bought the first in a series of Zeppelin dirigible airships in 1907. In 1910, the first planes were added to the army, and a Naval Air Service (NAS) was founded the following year. In 1912, the army's air arm was turned into the Military Aviation Service (MAS), though this remained separate from the NAS.

Around that same time, the Italians made the first practical use of air power during their 1911-12 invasion of Libya. During this campaign, a small number of aircraft were used to reconnoiter the enemy, direct artillery, and drop bombs. Still, the Italians lacked the resources to build a substantial air force, and as a result, Germany was fast becoming the global leader. By 1914, the NAS had 36 aircraft and the MAS had 250. In only five years, military planes had gone from non-existent to a significant and sizable fighting force, one whose potential had been demonstrated in the field by the Italians. Most of Germany's competitors had only around 50 aircraft, compared with their 300.

Even as planes were being manufactured at increasing rates, training for pilots remained primitive. Without the experience of extensive aerial combat, there was little understanding of the maneuvers a plane could make or the problems it would face when pushed to its limits. There was no body of tactical or flying knowledge to draw upon, and no philosophy of aerial warfare. Furthermore, the pilots themselves were drawn from the officer corps, meaning they were mostly bored young men looking for a bit of excitement. The high risk of accidents in these new flying machines contributed to a culture of boisterous thrill-seeking that gave them a poor reputation with the rest of the military.

With few flying instructors, no proper training regime, and planes unable to be taken up in poor weather, the pilots often had little flying experience. Some went into the war with as little as 17 hours of flying time under their belts, but they were young, daring and enthusiastic about the new form of warfare in which they were to play a part. Just as importantly, in comparison with other nations, the German air force was ready for war when it came.

Rickenbacker's Early Years

"When I look up and see the sun shining on the patch of white clouds up in the blue, I begin to think how it would feel to be up somewhere above it winging swiftly thought the clear air, watching the earth below, and the men on it, no bigger than ants." – Eddie Rickenbacker

Edward Rickenbacker was born on October 8, 1890, in Columbus, Ohio to Swiss German immigrants who instilled in their son a strong work ethic and a love for his country. The National Park Service describes his boyhood home: "Around 1893-95 William Rickenbacker built the first part of this simple, 1 1/2-story, L-shaped, gable-roofed dwelling. His son 'Eddie,' while growing up here, developed his interest in automobiles and airplanes, and this remained his only permanent home until well after World War I. ... It was 'Eddie' who eventually paid off the mortgage on this house. ...initially the house consisted of two downstairs rooms and two attic rooms. Probably around 1900 'Eddie' helped add a room and a half, apparently the north ell, and helped make a cellar. ... The low foundation is sandstone. ... Roofing shingles in an imbricated pattern appear original. A shed dormer with two windows and a central red brick chimney with corbeled cap top the main roof, while another red brick chimney surmounts the ell."

Like all children, Rickenbacker left behind more than one sign of his time in the house. "Next to the north door lies a bulkhead cellar door, which sits on a stone and concrete base, wherein the initials 'E. V. R.' are crudely traced. On the first floor, the dwelling consists of three rooms and a bath. Either two or 2 1/2 rooms occupy the attic loft, and a room and crawl space complete the basement. ... Just north of the house stands a one-story shed. Here young Rickenbacker may have undertaken his first mechanical experiments. The structure has green-painted clapboard siding, probably similar to that which covered the house originally, and it has wooden quoins."

The Auburn University website dedicated to Rickenbacker's papers explained the hardships Eddie and his parents endured during his childhood: "After 1893, William Rickenbacker operated his own construction company, but the family remained mired in poverty. Elizabeth Rickenbacker managed to save up enough money to buy two adjacent lots on East Livingston Avenue shortly after Eddie's birth. Against William's wishes, Elizabeth sold one lot and began building a house with two rooms and a loft on the other lot. The family moved into the house in 1893. They later added on a kitchen with another loft above. The house had no electricity, running water or indoor plumbing. Eddie recalled that most of the land surrounding their home on the outskirts of Columbus was used for growing vegetables and pasturing goats. William was a stern disciplinarian, present- and practical-minded, and Elizabeth instilled in Eddie a great reverence for religion, attributes that seemed to form the nucleus of Eddie's personality. Eddie remained close to his mother until her death in 1946."

As a little boy, he loved to take things apart and try to find ways to reconfigure them, guided always by his father's admonition that a "machine has to have a purpose." However, he was not always under his father's feet, or in his charge, as C.V. Glines pointed out in the January 1999 issue of *Aviation History*: "Young Rickenbacker was admittedly a bad boy who smoked at age 5 and headed a group of mischievous youngsters known as the Horsehead Gang, but he was imbued with family values by frequent applications of a switch to his posterior by his strict father. One of his father's axioms that he followed all his life was never to procrastinate. At age 8, he had his first brush with death when he led his gang down a slide in a steel cart into a deep gravel pit. The cart flipped over on him and laid his leg open to the bone."

Eddie's mother noted, "In boyhood, as in manhood, thought and action with Eddie were inseparable. I never saw its like. But his imagination—and he had aplenty—I'm sure it never soared to battles in the sky... Yes, he was a very, very mischievous boy, but never a bad boy. ... Neither his father nor I had the slighted turn for mechanics. There isn't a trace of it in the family, which came a generation ago to America from Switzerland. Yet it was only when busy with his hands making something that he stayed indoors and out of mischief."

Though it may have saved his life, tragedy brought a sudden end to Rickenbacker's childish mischief after his father died when he was just 12 years old. Auburn University explains, "Though his older brother (also named William) worked full-time, Eddie decided it was his job to support the family. He knew his mother and brother would oppose him, so he decided to present them with a fait accompli. He lied about his age to circumvent the child-labor laws and got a night job as a helper at the Federal Glass Factory. In a few weeks he quit to take a day job at the Buckeye Steel Casting Company. From there he worked in a beer factory, a bowling alley, a cemetery monument yard, and with the Pennsylvania Railroad as an apprentice. He was unhappy and viewed every job only as a way to make money for his family."

Fortunately for the young teen, change was just around the corner. According to Glines, "Engines became young Rickenbacker's passion, and he found a job that changed his life in 1906 when he went to work for Lee Frayer, a race car driver and head of the Frayer-Miller Automobile Co. Frayer liked the scrawny, scrappy lad and let him ride in major races as his mechanic. Rick later went to work as a salesman for the Columbus Buggy Co., which was then making Firestone-Columbus automobiles. He joined automobile designer Fred Duesenberg in 1912 and struck out on his own as a race car driver. He soon established a reputation as a daring driver and won some races — but not without numerous accidents and narrow escapes. After each crash he telegraphed his mother, telling her not to worry."

Frayer

Duesenberg

Rickenbacker at the 1915 American Grand Prize in San Francisco

Rickenbacker loved racing and competed in the first four races run at what would one day become the famous Indianapolis Motor Speedway. Indeed, he might have remained in racing until he retired, or died in one of the fiery crashes that claimed so many lives in the early years of the sport, had he not found another hobby. Gilnes explained, "While preparing for the Vanderbilt Cup Race in California in November 1916, he had his first ride in an aircraft — flown by Glenn Martin, who was beginning his own career as a pilot and aircraft manufacturer. Rickenbacker had a lifelong fear of heights, but he had not been apprehensive during the flight."

GLENN L. MARTIN

Martin

Rickenbacker may have been drawn to flying, but racing still owned his heart. As it turned out, his desire to purchase a new and better car nearly derailed his future career. He later testified, "I went to England to purchase a Sunbeam…I secured passports and on arrival in Liverpool I was questioned by the authorities there, the British Intelligence Bureau…I was ordered to stay on the boat that was going to be returned…they were looking for a German spy whose description I answered to a T, and with the name of Rickenbacker attached to me, of course they thought they had him; he sailed at the time I sailed."

Fortunately, Rickenbacker was able to use the same ingenuity that would later save lives to save his own reputation. He continued, "Christmas day came along and I persuaded the authorities…to let me spend Christmas day on land…I was able to get in touch with Mr. Coatalin, who was the directing manager of the Sunbeam Works, and he vouched for my status, and he got in communication with the Intelligence Bureau and they allowed me to proceed to London. … I was able to get in touch with English officers, and from their attitude and morale I realized that America would have to get into the war sooner or later."

With this understanding in mind, Rickenbacker recalled, "I decided to take up service with the British and join the British Aviation Corps;…I kept putting it off until the [American] diplomatic relations were severed with Germany, and then I decided to return to America immediately. ... I sailed on the 5th of February. All my papers were taken away from me...On arriving in America I was naturally full of enthusiasm about the war."

Rickenbacker knew that he and his friends had something unique to offer: "I felt that the boys in the racing game were better qualified for aviation than any other type of men we had. I also knew that the mechanics who had been interested in this sport and had experience with the high-speed motors and their development that aviation had not come to yet...so I thought it would be a good plan if I could to organize the racers who had been racing on land, as pilots, and the mechanics as enlisted personnel and have the Government supply the necessary physical personnel to bring about this organization... And there was no appropriation allotted for any such project, and I was also discouraged to the extent that they said that the more a man knew about motors the worse off he was so far as aviation was concerned, because he would pay too much attention to the motor and not enough to the flying and fighting."

War in the Sky

"We convinced him quickly that the possibility of war was absolutely nil and continued our festivity. On the next day we were ordered to take the field." – Manfred von Richthofen

In the fall of 1914, war broke out across Europe, and whether it was through miscalculation or a sense of inevitability, the great powers descended into a conflict that many had long expected. In a short while, the war spanned nearly the whole continent, sucked in other countries around the globe, and over the course of four years took millions of lives.

Indeed, the initial weeks of the war did not go as the generals had planned. The Germans' Schlieffen Plan, meant to be a fast strike to take out France before attacking Russia, was halted by the Allied Powers, creating the terrible and now iconic trench warfare for which World War I is most vividly remembered. As the infantry dug themselves into defensive trenches, cavalrymen such as von Richthofen found themselves worse than useless in the face of machine-guns and entangling barbed wire, and the expected war of maneuver became one of slow, grinding carnage.

Meanwhile, in the skies above the Western Front, the MAS were facing their first tests as Germany's air force. At the start of the war the aircraft were ill-equipped for combat mostly because the idea that planes might somehow fight was still a novel one, and the adaptations had not yet been developed that would allow the aerial battles later in the war. Aircraft were used almost entirely for reconnaissance, allowing generals to gain unprecedented levels of information about enemy movements. Such intelligence allowed the French to counter German movements in what became the Battle of the Marne, ending Germany's hopes for victory through the Schlieffen plan. Similarly, in the east, German planes were vital in tracking, encircling and destroying Russian forces at Tannenberg.

Some armies, such as the French, saw air intelligence as a strategic matter, with aircraft capable mainly of identifying enemy forces before battle and contributing to advanced preparations. The Germans, on the other hand, believed that aircraft could provide tactical information once battle had commenced. Pilots such as Oswald Boelcke, Germany's first great aerial officer, would fly over enemy positions in two-seat aircraft with a spotter in the back, identifying Allied positions and using colored lights to direct the fire of artillery on the ground.

Spotting took on great importance because of the growing range and power of artillery. Much of the fire from the great guns was aimed indirectly, since the gunners could not see their targets and thus relied on intelligence from others to direct them. Maps of enemy-held territory were often woefully inadequate to start with, and with the need to know where moving enemy formations were positioned, the business gained an added complexity, but aircraft could cut through this by providing up-to-date intelligence on enemy positions and send it back to the gun batteries which were lobbing shells over their own front lines.

That said, the use of aircraft to carry weapons began early on. Bombs were dropped on Paris in August 1914, and Zeppelins bombed Belgian forces as the Germans advanced on Liège. On the other side, British pilots destroyed a Zeppelin on the ground at Düsseldorf. This was bombing at its most simple; the explosives kept on hooks on the side of the machines and dropped by a crew member by hand. These small forays into aerial bombardment barely even hinted at the bombing campaigns to come.

Picture of a Zeppelin during the war

Picture of a crater left by a Zeppelin bomb in Paris during the war

The Zeppelins, slow and large as they were, proved to be easy targets for fire from the ground, so they were too vulnerable for reconnaissance in the warzone. Instead, they were used for the task of bombing England's eastern ports and London in an attempt to disrupt military supplies. This left the planes to fight for control of the skies over the Western front. From the start, pilots from opposing sides tried to take each other out and ensure their side's advantage in aerial intelligence, but since the machines were not equipped with weapons themselves, pilots initially carried hand weapons to fire from the cockpit or try to get above the enemy and drop projectiles. Flying at speeds up to 70 miles per hour and heights of up to 4,000 feet, these were not the fast-moving dogfights that would become a staple of later warfare, but by the standards of the time, these were exhilarating heights and speeds.

In rushing winds, men fought to steady themselves and draw a bead on the enemy in what started out as little more than sport between like-minded fliers but soon turned into a bitter battle for survival. It quickly became apparent that changes would be needed in the battle for aerial supremacy, and two different styles of plane emerged. On the one hand, there were the traditional two-seater crafts used for reconnaissance and the emerging art of bombing, with one man piloting while another took observations or dropped munitions. On the other hand, there were the fast single-seater scouts, designed to patrol the skies, chase away enemy planes and provide their side with aerial superiority. These new scouting planes needed forward firing guns so that the pilots could aim and fire without taking their attention off where they were going, but this created a problem, as guns mounted on the body of the plane were prone to shooting off their own propellers and taking them out before they could do any damage to the enemy, while those mounted high above the body were hard to aim, fire and unjam.

The French were the first to tackle the problem by designing a propeller reinforced with steel wedges to deflect the bullets, but it was far from a perfect solution. The bullets could still damage the propellers, and by sending them flying in every direction, the mechanism risked deflecting a bullet back at the pilot. In 1915, the MAS solved this problem and thus immediately gained a technological advantage over their opponents. Dutch engineer Anthony Fokker's interrupter gear stopped the gun from firing when a propeller blade was in front of it, but the gear allowed it to keep firing in the split seconds in between. This meant that for the first time, planes could be mounted with an automatic weapon that would shoot straight ahead, targeted in the same direction that the pilot was guiding the plane, and which did not risk shooting off the plane's own propeller or filling the pilot's face with rogue lead.

Fokker

As a result, starting in July 1915 with the Fokker E.I plane, German aircraft became war machines in their own right. Fokker's new aircraft was not only mounted with a superior weapon, it could also go faster and higher than most craft then in the skies. For the next six months, Germany had aerial superiority thanks to these planes, and aircraft production accelerated fast to meet the needs of the increasingly vital MAS and NAS. Having entered the war with a few hundred aircraft, Germany produced another 1,350 in 1914 and rising to 19,750 in 1917, a 15-fold increase in just three years.

Picture of a Fokker E.1

The tactics of aerial combat were also developing fast, and with its consequences of victory or death, fighting provided a good motive to learn better approaches fast. Oswald Boelcke, who without official permission had taken Fokker's plane for its first real outing, took the lead in developing the tactics that would make the Fokker plane invaluable. Staying on the German side of the lines, he used clouds and the glare of the sun to disguise his approach before shooting enemy planes down with short, accurate bursts of fire at close range. He paid attention not just to the workings of his machine but to those of his opponents, learning the design and limitations of captured Allied planes and determining the capabilities of their guns and where their blind spots lay. He also collaborated with the German anti-aircraft gunners on the ground, who provided him with warning shots when he was in danger and covering fire when he was under attack.

Boelcke

One of Boelcke's colleagues, Max Immelmann, added a sophisticated high speed maneuver to the German arsenal. The Immelmann turn, the first true air-to-air tactical maneuver, allowed the Fokker planes to attack their enemies again and again in quick succession, adding to their dominance as long as the enemy flew inferior planes. Its success helped earn its inventor his nickname "The Eagle of Lille," but this superiority only lasted until the following spring, when the Allied Powers developed and installed their own version of the Fokker technology. With that adaptation, the maneuver that had given Germans dominance now became a hazard to its own users.

Immelmann

Furthermore, Boelcke and Immelmann introduced the formation which has been the basis of fighter groups ever since: the pair of fighters. Boelcke realized that hunting out targets required a dangerous amount of attention; after all, while he was focused on stalking a single plane, others could approach without him noticing it. This meant the tactics which brought him success were also putting his life in danger. He therefore teamed up with Immelmann, the two guarding and protecting each other. The radios of the time were too heavy and cumbersome to install in an aircraft, so the pilots signaled to each other by waggling the wings of their planes, with Boelcke as the leader deciding when to attack and when to break off.

In January 1916, Immelmann and Boelcke, the first great heroes of aerial warfare, both received the Pour le Mérite awards, the highest honor in Germany, after shooting down their 8th enemy aircraft. They had become symbols of German dominance in the skies, but their planes, like those of their German comrades, were being used purely defensively, assigned to reconnaissance and spotter balloon squadrons to provide them with defense. They were out-shooting the Allied Powers, preventing them from gaining advantages, but not helping to push German troops forward.

1916 also saw a period in which technological advances gave the Allied Powers the upper hand. The Allies threw hundreds of pilots into supporting the bloody ground offensive on the Somme, and in doing so greatly supported their war effort. The British were hurling men and planes into the meat grinder, putting little effort into providing training and experience before they did so, but in the broader scope of the war, this was supporting their aims.

Later in 1916, the Germans regained the edge with the Albatros D.III plane, and the see-saw of military technological advantage swayed back and forth. Industrial programs were increasingly important when it came to providing both new technology and large amounts of material for aerial combat, and the Germans were not yet suffering from the shortages that would later hamper them.

The Albatros D.III

Boelcke's tactics were now fundamental for German military fliers. Pilots gained the advantage before they even entered combat, attacking from above with the sun to their backs. Shooting was in short bursts at close range, ignoring the instinct to fill the sky with a wild spray of bullets. When attacked, pilots did not run but turned towards their attackers, facing them head on to remove their advantage. It was an approach that required both calculation and daring, a perfect fit for men like Boelcke and von Richthofen.

Other innovations included the adoption of large formations of fighter aircraft. This started out as an Allied innovation to protect their planes from the technologically superior Fokkers, new models of which were now being produced. The Germans responded by forming squadrons of first 6 and then 14 planes, with Boelcke put in charge of a formation each time. It was on his suggestion that the German command formed the elite Jadgstaffeln units (or Jasta as they became known), large squadrons of top fliers whose purpose was to hunt Allied air formations and take them out of the skies. August 1916 saw the creation of the first two such formations: Jasta 1 under Hauptmann Zander and Jasta 2 under Boelcke himself. Such was his standing that he was allowed to hand pick his pilots, and while putting them together, Boelcke met young Lieutenant Manfred von Richthofen.

Eventually, Richthofen joined Boelcke's "Hunting Pack", and his reputation would eventually come to surpass that of his commander, but at the same time, it's only fair to point out that Richthofen's rise to prominence came in part because of the loss of the greats who had come before him. Death was common for fliers, and often terrible. There were no parachutes, and the best hope of surviving a damaged plane was a risky crash landing. If the plane caught fire then the pilot would often jump to his death rather than die in a cockpit inferno. These young officers were avoiding the now infamous horrors of trench warfare, but they faced their own sort of terror.

Immelmann, who in the early days achieved as many victories as his flying partner, died when his machine fell apart in the air in 1916. Boelcke, after a hugely successful autumn with his enlarged squadron and new Albatros plane, died in October 1916 when he crashed into another plane while diving towards an Allied aircraft.

With the deaths of Immelmann and Boelcke, Germany had lost her first great aerial heroes, but another was coming to take their place.

The Red Baron Flies

"My dear Excellency! I have not gone to war to collect cheese and eggs, but for another purpose." – Manfred von Richthofen

"There are some moments in one's life which tickle one's nerves particularly and the first solo-flight is among them." – Manfred von Richthofen

A certain glamour had quickly attached itself to aerial combat and the pilots who took part in it. The newspapers were clamoring for heroes to praise in a war largely fought through terrible, anonymous death by artillery bombardment and the dirty, unglamorous combat of trench warfare. Fighter pilots were an obvious exception, consisting of young men with uniquely modern skills, using the latest military technology, and fighting duels to the death in the clear blue skies above Flanders. Whatever the reality of their experience, the press leapt upon the fliers as heroes they could glorify in the midst of history's least glorious war.

All the while, the casualty rate of pilots remained ghastly. With parachutes only adopted near the end of the war, and men often killed when they crashed due to injuries or damaged craft, the turnover of pilots was horrific. New fliers had little time to adjust before being thrown straight into the war to fill the gaps, making it all the more likely that they would die before they could become skilled enough to survive. Exhaustion and pride affected the judgment of more experienced fliers, and even most of the great aces died in combat, but this harsh reality was not reported in the press, and for a cavalry officer deprived of the glories of mounted warfare, riding an aircraft suddenly looked very appealing.

Von Richthofen understood the difference between media accounts and reality, noting, "All the papers contained nothing but fantastic stories about the war. However, for several months we had been accustomed to war talk. We had so often packed our service trunks that the whole thing had become tedious." However, he also dreaded his time on the Eastern front and the lack of combat, complaining, "In the heat of the Russian summer a sleeping car is the most horrible instrument of martyrdom imaginable."

Thus, he transferred from the cavalry to the MAS in May 1915. Starting out as a probationary observer, he took a brief training course at Cologne, the kind of training available when training materials were so scant and pilots so desperately needed at the front. According to one contemporary, von Richthofen described his first experience in the air to him: "I had been told the name of the place to which we were to fly and I was to direct the pilot. At first we flew straight ahead, then the pilot turned to the right, then left. I had lost all sense of direction over our own aerodrome!...I didn't care a bit where I was, and when the pilot thought it was time to go down, I was disappointed. Already I was counting down the hours to the time we could start again..."

His first duties were in a reconnaissance flight on the Russian front. Then at the end of August 1915 he was transferred to Ostend where he joined a bombing unit, and in September he was moved on again, this time to Champagne. Referring to this time, he said, "One can become enthusiastic over anything. For a time I was delighted with bomb throwing. It gave me a tremendous pleasure to bomb those fellows from above."

As his quotes indicate, the experiences as an observer frustrated him. While occupying the second seat in a cumbersome two-seater reconnaissance or bombing plane, there was no opportunity to engage in combat with the Allied pilots, or to experience the thrill and glamour of aerial combat. For a young man brought up in the proud Prussian military tradition, this was maddening, and he longed to get behind the controls of the single-seater planes dueling with each other above the battlefield.

Ironically, von Richthofen showed little promise as a flier and responded poorly to training from one of his former pilots, but there was always a need for more men to fly these planes, so in November 1915 he was sent to join the flying school at Döberitz near Berlin. What von

Richthofen lacked in natural skill he made up for in dogged determination and the will to become what he wanted, and he ultimately passed the pilots' tests. Thus, in March 1916, after having proved himself worthy of being a fighter pilot, von Richthofen returned to the Western front and joined the Second Fighter Squadron at Verdun. He was now the pilot of a two-seater plane, not where he wanted to be but well on his way.

Von Richthofen's driving ambition was to become one of Boelcke's pilots, serving and learning under the famous fighter ace. He wrote about it in his letters home, and he took the first available opportunity to undertake a test flight in a Fokker single-seater plane like the ones flown by his hero. Still, he was no Boelcke, and a combination of bad luck and his own lack of natural aptitude held him back. Making a forced landing after the engine failed, von Richthofen reduced the Fokker to scrap.

Given his performance to date, it is no surprise that Richthofen was sent back to pilot two-seaters on the Eastern front, a less challenging theatre of aerial combat, but this actually proved fortuitous because it was there that he finally met his hero Boelcke, who was visiting von Richthofen's brother. It is hard to tell what led Boelcke to invite Manfred von Richthofen into the hand-picked squadron he was then assembling, given that the young man had shown no great aptitude as a fighter pilot. In fact, his only experience with the planes he would be flying had ended with a crash landing, and he had been relegated to the less glamorous and less challenging front of the war. Most pilots in the German air force were probably eager to fly under Boelcke, yet he chose this obscure and struggling pilot.

It would be easy to dismiss the decision as stemming from Boelcke's connection with von Richthofen's brother, but there was clearly more to it. Manfred had demonstrated incredible perseverance in pushing to become a fighter pilot, and his self-confidence was unflinching, out of all proportion to his actual achievements. In the same vein, he was fearless in the face of the hazards of flying, and while he had little experience behind the trigger of a Fokker's machine-gun, he was an excellent shot with sporting guns. In fact, von Richthofen once bragged, "I should have been delighted had it come to a fight. I felt absolutely sure of myself with a pistol in my hand." In short, he had the ideal qualities to impress a fellow young man of Germany's aristocratic officer class.

Whatever the reasons, Manfred von Richthofen was invited to join the most prestigious air unit of the war to date, Boelcke's new Jasta 2, and the unit saw the first in its long string of successes on September 17, 1916, during the fighting on the Somme. In this fighting, von Richthofen scored his own first success, shooting down a British F.E.2b of Number 11 Squadron and mortally wounding Second Lieutenant Morris and Lieutenant Rees, the men in the plane. Like Boelcke, von Richthofen brought a hunter's instincts to the skies. Ruthless, patient, and calculating, he stalked his prey through the air, using sun, wind and cloud cover to gain an advantage of position and descend upon them with deadly power and suddenness. The Red

Baron once asserted, "During my whole life I have not found a happier hunting ground than in the course of the Somme Battle. In the morning, as soon as I had got up, the first Englishmen arrived, and the last did not disappear until long after sunset. Boelcke once said that this was the El Dorado of the flying men."

As it turned out, Von Richthofen took part in the battle on October 28 in which his commander and hero was killed. Boelcke and another pilot, Erwin Boehme, were diving after a British D.H.2 plane of Number 24 Squadron, but another D.H.2, under fire from von Richthofen, burst across their line of sight. Boelcke banked away and Boehme swerved, resulting in the two colliding with each other. The struts and upper wing of Boelcke's plane collapsed and broke away, the plane fell into a spin, and it crashed into the ground near Bapaume. In the whirling chaos of combat, Richthofen had unwittingly played a part in bringing about Boelcke's demise.

Jasta 2 was renamed Jasta Boelcke by imperial decree, in honor of the man who had done so much to shape Germany's fledgling air force. Lieutenant Stephen Kirmaier took command following the master's death, but he too died in action less than a month later and was followed by Hauptmann Waltz.

Meanwhile, von Richthofen soon built up an impressive string of victories. On November 23, he took down one of the leading British flying aces, Victoria Cross holder Major L. G. Hawker, his 11th kill. With Hawker crashing behind enemy lines, Richthofen was able to salvage one of his plane's guns and kept it as a proud trophy. It was a credo in line with one of his most famous quotes: "I honored the fallen enemy by placing a stone on his beautiful grave."

Hawker

The Flying Circus

Richthofen (in the plane) with Jasta 11

"Everything depends on whether we have for opponents those French tricksters or those daring rascals, the English. I prefer the English. Frequently their daring can only be described as stupidity. In their eyes it may be pluck and daring." – Manfred von Richthofen

"He fought until he landed. When he had come to the ground I flew over him at an altitude of about thirty feet in order to ascertain whether I had killed him or not. What did the rascal do? He took his machine-gun and shot holes into my machine." – Manfred von Richthofen

No longer under Boelcke's tutelage, Manfred von Richthofen was emerging as a leading pilot in his own right, and by early 1917 Manfred von Richthofen's star was on the rise. On January 4, he had shot down his 16th plane, making him one of Germany's leading fliers and a popular hero at home. He was awarded the order *Pour le Mérite* for his achievements, and by the end of the month he was commanding his own squadron, Jasta 11. His instructions for his men were simple: "Aim for the man and don't miss him. If you are fighting a two-seater, get the observer first; until you have silenced the gun, don't bother about the pilot."

April 1917 was one of the most successful phases of the war for von Richthofen. He and his men brought down dozens of British planes in what their opponents referred to as "bloody April," and in just five days from April 4-8, the British lost 75 planes, with 19 men killed, 13 wounded, and 73 reported missing. But the most significant single engagement of this fighting came on April 28, when British flier Captain W. Leefe Robinson, a man who had earned the Victoria Cross for shooting down a Zeppelin, led six Bristol F2B fighters of Number 48 Squadron across enemy lines. The Bristol was the great new hope of the Royal Flying Corps, a heavily armed two-seater plane with a forward firing Vickers machine-gun and a pair of Lewis guns operated by the observer in the rear seat.

A sturdy, powerful plane, it held great promise for the British, but their unfamiliarity with it would lead to an unfortunate early outing. The Bristols had barely crossed the front line when five German Albatros planes, led by von Richthofen, descended upon them. The British might have fine new planes, but the Germans were familiar with their own machines and had the tactical advantage. Almost immediately von Richthofen took out the first Bristol, sending it spinning towards the ground. A vicious dogfight ensued, during which three more of the Bristols were shot down, and the last two, one piloted by Leefe Robinson, staggered away. Nonetheless, the captain's plane was too badly damaged to make it back to the British lines, forcing him to land his bullet-torn machine in German territory, where he was captured and spent the rest of the war a prisoner. Von Richthofen had turned the first outing of the glorious new British flying machine into a total disaster.

Including the engagement on April 28, von Richthofen shot down 21 British planes that month, and after the engagement with Leefe Robinson's planes, he was able to report that the Bristol fighter was no use to the Allies. This would prove to be a moment of over confidence; once the British got experience with their new planes they put them to good use, and they would turn the tide of battle later in the summer.

The success of Bloody April came in part from a shift in German military tactics towards defense in depth. Reports from anti-aircraft guns created an early warning system that gave the Germans notice of Allied air attacks, and they were able to prevent almost all French reconnaissance flights, severely hampering enemy intelligence and artillery operations. By now, scout planes were being used in a variety of roles, including those originally reserved for the slower planes. They fought other aircraft for domination of the skies, dropped bombs, strafed enemy troops with their guns, and provided reconnaissance of enemy formations, the last activity often being combined with the others.

The victory to which Richthofen and his men contributed led to mutinies in the French army which endangered the whole Allied war effort, and by the end of April, von Richthofen had shot down a total of 52 planes, killing 56 men and wounding or leading to the capture of 26 more. This partly came down to hard work; he would take his squadron up twice as often as many other commanders, keeping them in constant action.

Still, despite the month's successes, the end of April brought a change in German tactics, led by General Ernst von Hoeppner, who had taken over command of the air force the previous October. Starting on April 30, groups of 20 planes, formed by bringing together separate units, swept the battlefield. Temporary at first, these formations impressed the command, and they soon recalled von Richthofen from leave to command the first permanent *Jagdgeschwader* formation.

Ernst von Hoeppner

Hermann Thomsen (German Air Service Chief of Staff), von Richthofen, and Hoeppner

Von Richthofen's Jagdgeschwader 1 was made up of four Jastas - numbers 4, 6, 11 and 10 - and it was a linchpin of the German war effort. Based at Courtrai, they were responsible for ensuring German air supremacy above whichever part of the front the High Command dictated. Deployed around the line wherever they were most needed, they were given resources available to few other units, including a large motor pool to take them from place to place and a corrugated iron headquarters that could be disassembled and reassembled in a few hours, their homes moving with them. Military celebrities to the Germans and a terrifying menace to the Allies, they appeared suddenly and without warning all along the battlefront.

Success also gave Richthofen and his men more leeway than others, and the fame and spectacle of the squadron only grew with their flamboyance. Ever since his days in Jasta Boelcke, von Richthofen had flown a plane painted entirely in red, earning him his legendary nickname and at least a bit of derision among other German fliers. Von Richthofen relayed one other German pilot's anecdote: "In the Squadron to which he belonged there was a rumor that the Red Machine was occupied by a girl, by a kind of Jeanne d'Arc. He was intensely surprised when I assured him that the supposed girl was standing in front of him. He did not intend to make a joke. He was actually convinced that only a girl could sit in the extravagantly painted machine."

Von Richthofen encouraged similarly bright schemes among the fliers of Jasta 11. He now extended this to Jagdgeschwader 1. Starting out as an improvement on colored tassels used to identify a squadron leader's plane, the decoration of planes became a phenomenon in its own right, despite the development of patterned fabrics meant to make aircraft harder to spot. Von Richthofen let the rest of the squadron paint their planes however they wanted as long as no one else used his all red scheme. Variations on their leader's colors were popular, with one pilot having a red plane with black control surfaces, while Richthofen's own brother Lothar chose a similar scheme, but with yellow instead of black.

The spectacular colors and roaming lifestyle earned the squadron the nickname of the Flying Circus, and their distinctive planes let the enemy know that they were facing Germany's deadliest pilots. Everyone in the air force wanted to associate themselves with the glamour of the Circus, and before long, other squadrons were painting their aircraft bright colors in imitation of the famed Red Baron and his men. At the same time, however, the Germans were fighting a defensive war in the air, generally outnumbered but never outmatched in skills and technology, and von Richthofen did not indulge in the sportsmanlike attitudes of the early war fliers but fought with ruthless efficiency. It was his job to destroy as many of the enemy as possible while losing as few of his own men as he could. For all the allure of glory, he was willing to withdraw when appropriate. Allied flights ensured that he was never short of targets, and he did not have to take risks to find the enemy or bring them down. He conceded, "There were sometimes from forty to sixty English machines, but unfortunately the Germans were often in the minority. With them quality was more important than quantity."

Realistic about the disadvantages, von Richthofen selected and developed his officers for the same attitudes that served him so well. He encouraged patience, confidence, and an understanding of what was proportionate in their form of war. They became one of the most efficient fighting forces around, elusive and deadly, appearing where they could be most effective only to fade away again into the skies. In conjunction with that, his approach to the training of new fliers was a rigorous one. On joining his squadron they spent up to two weeks on practice flights, until he was content that they could perform the basic maneuvers of his aerial group. They then joined the formation in the air, but were expected to withdraw the first few times they encountered the enemy. He studied their strengths and weaknesses, identifying what role each one would play in the squadron, expecting nothing but the best from his men.

Von Richthofen himself was central to the success of the battles he fought in. Leading from the front, he contributed to the hard-hitting initial impact. He then ascended to oversee the fighting from above, darting back down to assist inexperienced pilots who found themselves in trouble and acting as a central point around which the squadron could regroup. He also ensured that the pilots took part in thorough debriefings after every flight so that they could make the most of the learning opportunities the action provided. Von Richthofen also placed a great deal of emphasis on the planes' guns and their maintenance, because pilots themselves were responsible for ensuring that their guns operated smoothly, just as a hunter has to take care of his weapons. If they jammed in action, then this was the pilot's own fault, not that of the ground crew.

Increasingly large formations inevitably led to larger aerial battles, to the point that dozens of planes would engage in combat in an area a few miles across, with groups bursting upwards as they tried to outmaneuver each other and gain the advantage of height. Planes would rise and fall, hurtle upwards and dive back down, break off and then return to the fight. The air roared with the noise of their engines and their guns. As this description suggests, even though the planes flew to battle in formation, once combat was joined it soon became a chaotic mass of individual planes pursuing each other through the sky. Pilots supported one another, but the need for fast maneuvering outweighed the benefits of keeping in formation. These were nerve-wracking engagements in which one, two or three planes would engage an enemy craft at a time, forming dozens of individual dogfights amid a wider whirl of battle.

Von Richthofen took part in one such battle on July 6, 1917. Leading a group of 8 Albatroses, he closed in on a group of slow British planes. The British formed a defensive circle covering each other's blind spots, giving them a better defense, but von Richthofen persisted, and the fighting drew in other pilots from both sides. Two British and four German planes fell from the skies around him as the deadly combat progressed, and just as von Richthofen was maneuvering to close with the British, disaster struck. He and a British two-seater FE2d piloted by Captain Donald Cunnell flew head-on straight towards each other, guns blazing. Less than a hundred yards apart, a bullet fired by Cunnell's observer, Second Lieutenant Albert Woodbridge, hit von Richthofen in the head. The bullet left Richthofen temporarily blinded and half paralyzed, and he lost control of his plane, which spiraled towards the ground as he fought for control first of his own body and then of his plane. At the last possible moment he regained some sight, just in time to make a crash landing behind friendly lines before passing out.

Richthofen's plane after the crash landing

Von Richthofen was rushed to hospital, where he was found to have suffered a fractured skull, but within weeks he was up and flying again, returning to duty on July 26. Not surprisingly, he had not had time to properly recover, and he suffered from headaches, dizziness and nausea as a result of the combat. His ability to fight was impaired, and his kill rate fell, but he was determined to be back in the war, which had begun to swing against his men. From September to November, he was persuaded to take leave to properly recover, but such rest did not suit him; though his brush with death had left him weakened mentally, the Red Baron could not sit out the fight. As he put it, "I have had an experience which might perhaps be described as being shot down. At the same time, I call shot down only when one falls down. Today I got into trouble but I escaped with a whole skin."

April 1917 had marked the absolute height of German aerial superiority, but the war in the air started to turn against the Germans in May. Though they still had better trained crews, they were once more put at a technological disadvantage because a new generation of British planes such as the Sopwith Camel outmatched even the Albatros. Despite the glamour of the flying aces, industrial production was just as important to victory, and with America contributing indirectly to the Allied war effort through its economic contributions, the Allies were able to produce more planes. Careful deployment of the Flying Circus somewhat countered this, allowing the Germans to gain the advantage of numbers in particular parts of the sky by better concentrating their aerial efforts, but across the broad sweep of the war, they were in danger of being overwhelmed by opponents who could more easily replace their lost planes and thus afford to throw them into battle after battle. The entrance of the Americans into the war in 1917, bringing to bear the full weight of their fast-growing industrial economy, meant that the pressure was only increasing.

Along with these developments, morale among the German pilots declined. Richthofen himself noted this in a letter to a friend in July 1917, writing, "No one wants to be a fighter pilot any more." Coming from the most famous man in the air, this is a sign of how desperate the situation had become, and why he felt such an urgent need to return to action after his near-fatal injury. He was central to the German air force, and recognized his own importance in keeping together an air service under desperate stress.

The German government recognized the importance of Richthofen and his fellow pilots' war in the air, so in the summer of 1917, they began the Amerikaprogramm to counter the impact of the war's latest participant. Under this plan, German industry was to produce 2,000 aircraft and 2,500 engines for them each month until January 1918. However, while it was a grand scheme, it was also an unrealistic one, and like many poorly planned industrial policies of the 20th century, it created problems that only ran counter to its goals. Under pressure, strikes broke out throughout the industry, and prices for aircraft soared. Standards of production declined as the factories hurried to meet this forced demand, producing sub-standard craft instead of failing to meet their targets by making better ones.

On August 28, 1917, Germany unveiled a new plane, the Fokker Dr.I triplane. Von Richthofen himself soon adopted the Triplane, and it became strongly associated with the mystique of the Red Baron. Highly maneuverable and with a great rate of climb, it sacrificed speed to achieve this level of agility. The Triplane proved highly effective for the Germans, who were fighting their defensive battles over their own territory, and its significant disadvantage in speed seldom became apparent. In the hands of the Flying Circus, the Triplane briefly provided a match for the newer Allied planes.

Oliver Thiele's picture of a replica of Richthofen's Fokker Dr.I triplane

However, the Triplane had a significant defect, one which became apparent as fighting heated up during the Battle of Cambrai that November. Now in almost constant service, the Triplane proved vulnerable to an internal weakness: in long dives, the canvas tended to tear away from the upper wing, often leading the whole structure to collapse. Good pilots were lost not to enemy fire but to their own planes giving way beneath them, and a plane that disintegrated in a dive was useless to an air force whose tactics involved diving from above against the enemy, and who were participating in the whirling, up and down melees that by then were taking place between a hundred or more planes on each side.

Given its problem, the Triplane was withdrawn from service, but von Richthofen had been impressed with its capabilities, so Anthony Fokker presented him with an improved and strengthened model. As a result, von Richthofen remained the pilot of this distinctive and often deadly plane.

It was a big enough challenge to produce thousands of aircraft, but finding the men to pilot them proved as difficult as manufacturing the machines themselves. The Germans had done better than the Allies in training their pilots, but the MAS now faced a terrible choice. On the one hand, they could pull men out of the training schools and reserves to fight on the front lines, shoring up the numbers in combat but harming training and strategic flexibility. On the other hand, they could maintain a robust infrastructure of well-trained pilots but leave the front line formations undermanned in the face of growing Allied numbers. The careful application of their own resources could only carry them so far under such circumstances.

This must have been a source of incredible frustration to men such as von Richthofen. They were the best fighting men in their field and raised to see this as the path to glory, but matters of supply and economics were robbing them of the victory that they felt should be theirs. However hard they tried, however much they pushed their aircraft, however many enemy pilots they shot down, the war was still being lost.

The Final Campaign

"Of course, with the increasing number of aeroplanes one gains increased opportunities for shooting down one's enemies, but at the same time, the possibility of being shot down one's self increases." – Manfred von Richthofen

"The English had hit upon a splendid joke. They intended to catch me or to bring me down." – Manfred von Richthofen

By 1918, Germany's fortunes in the skies were falling. An Allied blockade was throttling German industry, making it impossible to maintain levels of aircraft production, and the violence had also taken its toll. In the three years leading up to September 1918, the MAS lost 2,000 planes and 11,000 men, enough to wipe out the pre-war air force several times over. These difficulties reflected the wider picture of the war, during which Germany found itself out-produced by the Allied industrial machine.

In March 1918, Germany launched one last great offensive, using innovative tactics that relied on the air force to direct sudden, surprising, and accurate artillery bombardments at key moments. This was meant to throw the enemy off balance, creating opportunities for the German troops to rapidly exploit, again relying on superior intelligence. To support this plan, the number of aircraft on the Western front had been steadily increased, many coming from the Eastern front, and new units were formed until there were 77 Jasta, many of them grouped into larger formations.

Operation Michael began on March 21, 1918, and with that, concentration of resources was once more critical. Focused air and artillery resources put the Allies on the defensive, and the British, unable to coordinate their own artillery and air support, were ripped apart. For two whole days, the Germans dominated the skies, and at last von Richthofen and his comrades had the victory they had so long waited for, and which they felt they deserved. By March 24, the Allies had managed to reinforce their air squadrons facing the Operation Michael advance, but while more Allied aircraft meant more pressure on the Germans, they also meant more targets for von Richthofen, and so began his last great run of victories. On March 24, he led a squadron of 25 planes in a battle against 10 aircraft of the Royal Flying Corps' famous 56 Squadron, during which he brought down his 67th opponent. Over the next week, he brought down another seven enemy planes, including three in one day. He was once again the darling of the German media and the dread of the Allies, a pilot at the peak of his career.

Von Richthofen seemed unstoppable in the skies, but those who met him outside the blazing destruction of aerial combat saw a different man. With growing desperation, both sides were throwing their pilots and planes in to support their ground troops by attacking those of the enemy. Casualties were huge on both sides, but this was something that the Germans could ill afford, and the strain of combat was taking its toll on the Red Baron. Once a fiery young warrior, filled with energy and determined to achieve glory in the skies, the past three years of aerial warfare had ground him down. It's fair to wonder how that youthful ardor could have possibly remained when he had seen so many comrades die and inflicted so much death on the opposing fliers, not to mention his responsibilities leading an increasingly desperate fight under growing pressure. Moreover, no matter how many victories he racked up, the German economy simply could not provide them with the resources they needed.

Indeed, the nature of a flier's death haunted the Red Baron, who once discussed some of his experiences with a newspaper reporter: "The last ten I shot down burned. The one I got today burned too." A burning plane was among the most horrifying fates a pilot could face, with many leaping to their deaths rather than die that way. It is perhaps unsurprising that it obsessed a man who had brought down nearly 80 planes, and seen many more fall from the skies. Nor was he the only pilot to start obsessing over those fearful flames, but those other pilots were not the Red Baron, the hero at the heart of the German flying force, a national idol showing clear signs of emotional exhaustion.

Whatever he was feeling, von Richthofen continued to press on through the grueling struggle of Operation Michael, and he continued working on the maintenance and the future of his squadron. In between the fighting, he found time to visit other Jastas working with the 2nd Army, during which he recruited Ernst Udet to his squadron. This is indicative of von Richthofen's almost magical reputation; Udet was the commander of Jasta 37 and had already brought down 20 Allied planes, making him an ace and a flying star in his own right, but the chance to fly with von Richthofen was more than any German flier could resist. He transferred to the Flying Circus, and on his first flight he achieved yet another kill, shooting down a Sopwith Camel.

Udet

On April 20, half a dozen Fokkers led by von Richthofen intercepted a patrol of 12 Sopwith Camels under Captain Douglas Bell, accompanied by Major Richard Raymond-Barker, the commanding officer of the British 3 Squadron. Bell had lost half his group in the heavy clouds that obscured the battlefield, making for roughly even numbers in the fight, and the Red Baron quickly got onto Raymond-Barker's tail. Showing his by now legendary aerial marksmanship, von Richthofen hit the Major's plane. Its petrol tank exploded and it crashed to the ground, another of the fiery deaths with which the German was becoming obsessed. It was his 79th victory.

Moments later, von Richthofen scored his 80th victory, shooting down Second Lieutenant David Lewis, but the story is as remarkable for Lewis's survival as for the Red Baron reaching 80. Lewis had descended from a high position in pursuit of a blue Fokker, but now found himself pursued by von Richthofen and at a disadvantage because of the height he had lost. The German ace riddled Lewis's Camel with bullets, and the British airman was unable to shake him off. Bullets shattered the compass in front of Lewis's face, the liquid from inside fogging his goggles. The goggles themselves were then lost as another bullet tore through the elastic holding them on. Half-blinded by the rushing wind, Lewis saw his plane disintegrating around him, struts and control wires shattered by machine-gun fire. The bombardment only ended when Lewis's fuel tank caught fire and von Richthofen, certain that his enemy was out of the fight, turned in search of other targets.

Lewis now seemed to face the awful choice of so many men before him: die in his flaming plane or jump out and fall to his death. However, he saw another option; thousands of feet up in the air, he sent his machine into a nosedive, and as he hurtled towards the ground, the speed of his descent kept the flames from consuming him and his machine. 500 feet above the ground, the flames seemed to subside, so he tried to pull his plane onto a horizontal path to land, but the mangled controls barely responded, and he was only just able to pull level. He hit the ground at high speed and was thrown from his wrecked plane, finding himself near the burning remains of Major Raymond-Barkers' craft. Burned and bruised, Lewis staggered to his feet and hurried over to see if he could pull his comrade's body clear, but the flames were too intense. When he finally had time to rest, Lewis found bullet holes in his trouser leg and his sleeve.

The Red Baron's 80th victim had survived by the skin of his teeth, but von Richthofen celebrated this 80th victory as he returned to base, flying low over the German troops. They waved and flung their caps in the air in tribute to the ace, little knowing that by the next night they would be mourning his demise.

By the end of the Operation Michael offensive, the Germans had gained a staggering amount of territory, at least by the slow moving standards of the war, but their air force had taken huge losses. In January 1918, they had already been feeling the pain, losing approximately one man in every 17, and by the end of May, they were losing one pilot out of seven every month. These losses were terrible for the men around them and far exceeded what the training establishments could replace. Those who remained were spread even more thinly as a result of the territorial gains, with supply lines failing as they advanced from one airbase to the next, exhausted from dozens of fierce fights in support of the army. Still, morale among the fliers endured surprisingly well, buoyed up by the reputation and leadership of men such as the Red Baron.

Thus, it was somewhat ironic that as Operation Michael was petering out, von Richthofen had his final fight. Sunday, April 21, began much like any other day of the war. Von Richthofen was thinking about life beyond the war zone, planning a hunting trip with Joachim Wolff, another young pilot. Even on his days off, the Red Baron planned to go shooting, but at least that stage in the war would allow a day off. Von Richthofen and a small flight of six aircraft left their aerodrome around 10:30, the usual roar of engines and blaze of brightly colored wings ascending into a grim sky. In the air they joined one of the large German squadrons, forming a mixed group of Albatroses and Fokker triplanes.

Normally the Germans stayed behind their own lines, relying on the more aggressive tactics of the Allies to provide them with targets. Fighting on the defensive meant that the Germans had the advantage of support from their army's anti-aircraft guns, and that if they were shot down they would most likely land behind their own lines, avoiding capture by the enemy. Such captures didn't just matter because of the men either, because both sides could learn each other's technology by examining crashed aircraft. It was just such a crashed plane that had allowed Fokker to adapt the first French machine-gun mounted behind a propeller, and within days to turn this into his own interrupter gun, giving the Germans superior firepower earlier in the war.

However, the Circus went flying that day with a specific purpose, and one that was different from their usual missions. The German army was preparing for a ground offensive, and they wanted to make sure that the Allies did not know what was coming or where. British two-seater reconnaissance planes were being sent out over the lines to photograph and report on the German preparations, and von Richthofen's mission was to destroy such planes. Before taking to the skies he had given his pilots instructions to look out particularly for enemy two-seaters, the prey for their daily hunt

The wind that morning was against them. Usually blowing from the west, it could be relied on to carry the fighting further over German lines, ensuring that if they were shot down they would land in friendly territory, but on this day the wind was blowing from the east, out of Germany and towards the Allied lines. Moreover, the weather was cloudy with poor visibility, providing cover for the German squadron but also making it difficult for them to spot targets. This hindered navigation, though occasional glimpses of the ground below allowed the pilots to keep track of roughly where they were.

Around 10:45, while flying west along the valley of the Somme and over the front lines, Richthofen's fliers spotted a pair of R.E.8 planes from an Australian Flying Corps squadron photographing the front lines west of the village of Le Hamel, behind German lines. Four of the Circus planes descended to attack the R.E.8s, confident of their superiority in aerial combat. Dividing a squadron like this was a common tactic, keeping some planes in reserve where they would retain the advantage of height and surprise. It also meant that they could be used to pick off enemy craft that became damaged or cut off from the rest of their group.

Four German fighters against two unwieldy two-seater spotter planes must have seemed like more than enough, but the Australians handled their planes well, with the observers returning fire at close range. They brought down two of the Fokkers, while British anti-aircraft guns opened fire from the far side of the nearby battle lines. This anti-aircraft fire drew the attention of a formation of Camel planes led by Canadian Captain A. R. Brown of 209 Squadron. Drawing close, they spotted the two remaining German planes and closed to engage, only to spy the main German formation of brightly colored Fokkers waiting nearby.

Brown

Captain Brown's group was low on numbers, with two planes having broken off to pursue German reconnaissance planes and two more returning home with engine problems. This left his 8 planes outnumbered two to one, an opportunity that von Richthofen had no reason to resist, and fighting quickly commenced. As was usually the case, this broke into a set of small skirmishes between two or three pilots, and in the chaos, the Australian R.E.8s, ill-equipped for the fast-flying carnage of fighter combat, broke off and returned to Le Hamel to complete their work. Meanwhile, the wind carried the fighting west, with planes darting back and forth across the trenches, watched from below by the soldiers of both sides.

Above the pack, von Richthofen circled the fighting, looking for a target to pick off, and one soon appeared when a British Sopwith Camel broke away. The pilot, Second Lieutenant Wilfred R. May, was a relatively new pilot and had been given orders that, if he found himself caught up in a dogfight, he should break away when he could and fly home. His two machine guns having jammed, he left the fighting and headed out towards home. Seeing clear skies behind him he congratulated himself on getting safely out of the fray.

Just as he thought he was safe, May saw tracer fire flashing past him, and he then realized he had a bright red plane on his tail. Though he did not know it, he was being chased by the deadliest ace of the war, von Richthofen, in his customized scarlet Fokker. May zigzagged through the sky, his course carrying him across the lines, and in his attempts to lose the Red Baron, he flew close to the ground down the Somme Valley, but von Richthofen dogged his every move, waiting for the perfect opportunity to fire.

Meanwhile, Captain Brown had seen that May was in trouble and broke away from the rest of the fighting to chase after the brightly colored triplane on his comrade's tail, unaware of who he himself was hunting. Von Richthofen was equally unaware. The whole reason for flying in groups was that it was hard for a pilot, focused on chasing down a target, to pay attention to threats coming from his side or rear. Oblivious to the Canadian Captain bearing down on him from the cloudy sky, the German ace continued his deadly pursuit.

As all of this suggests, the Red Baron was breaking many of his own rules for how to fight. In chasing May, he allowed himself to become separated from the support of his squadron. He also followed his target close to the ground, losing the advantage of height. Even his machine-guns, for which he always said the pilot was responsible, suffered from jams. Perhaps he was just feeling lucky, or perhaps the strains of the war had damaged his keen edge. Whatever the case, Brown came out of a dive to von Richthofen's right, opening fire with his twin machine guns as soon as he was within range. The German ace, caught by surprise, turned in his seat to look towards Brown, who believed that he saw his target crumple in the cockpit. Content that he had dealt with the threat to May, Brown turned back towards the main fight, chasing away two more Fokkers that had been pursuing him.

While the truth of the matter will always remain disputed, Brown's attack may not have been fatal for von Richthofen. His plane kept going, apparently in pursuit of May, and Lieutenant D. L. Fraser, intelligence officer for the 11th Infantry Brigade, reported the continuing chase between the two planes, with the German pursuing the British plane. May himself would later say that he thought his own poor flying was the only thing that saved him, crediting his lack of skill and experience with making it impossible for the Red Baron to predict his course.

After Brown had broken away from his pursuit of the Red Baron, the Fokker zigzagged through the air down the Somme Valley and over the Allied lines, which made it a target for anti-aircraft batteries on the ground. Along the way, von Richthofen's plane was fired on by two Australian machine-gunners, Sergeant Cedric B. Popkin and Gunner R. F. Weston, of the 24th Machine Gun Company, whose guns had been placed in a wooded area near Corbie to provide anti-aircraft fire. Based on Lieutenant Fraser's report, it seems that this fire hit Richthofen's plane if not the man himself, because his course became more erratic. Gunners W. J. Evans and Robert Buie of the 53rd Battery of the 14th Australian Field Artillery Brigade also fired their Lewis anti-aircraft guns on the Red Baron's plane, which turned and started back towards the German lines after flying over Buie's position.

Picture of the 24th Machine Gun Company with Popkin second from the right in the middle row

Whoever was responsible, somewhere in the brief minutes of pursuing May, Richthofen had been mortally wounded by a bullet to the chest, and his plane crashed to the ground roughly two miles behind the British lines. When the Allies approached the scarlet plane, its once terrifying fuselage lying broken in a Somme Valley field, they found the pilot dead, but given that he had managed to land the plane at all, it's likely von Richthofen was still alive for at least a short while on the ground. Regardless, two weeks away from his 26th birthday, Germany's hero was carried, cold and dead, into an empty British hangar. The Red Baron's war was over.

The falling red eagle on the badge for 209 Squadron is a commemoration of the end of the Red Baron

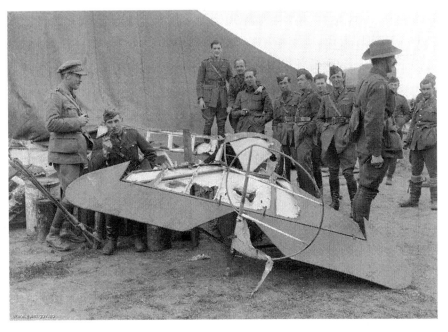

Allied soldiers pose with some of the wreckage from the Red Baron's plane

Having fallen behind enemy lines, Manfred von Richthofen was buried not by his friends but by his enemies, but the number of them that turned out to mark the occasion demonstrate the bonds that existed between the airmen of the two opposing sides and the high esteem in which the Red Baron was held even by the men he had so often tried to kill. A sense of old-fashioned honor existed among these knights of the skies, a respect for the skill and courage of their opponents, and perhaps there was an element of curiosity as well, with men wanting to be able to say that they had attended the funeral of such a celebrity and to be sure that their most deadly enemy really was in the ground. Von Richthofen was buried at Bertangles on the afternoon of April 22, with full military honors. His body was carried in a plain wooden coffin from the hangar where it had spent the night, solemnly transported on the shoulders of six R.A.F. officers. Placed on a hearse, it was followed by over 100 mourners to the graveside. There, the war's most famous fighter was lowered into the same Somme Valley dirt that had swallowed hundreds of thousands of humble infantrymen over the preceding years.

A picture of von Richthofen's funeral procession

An English chaplain carried out the burial rites, following the words and gestures of a Church of England service in the simple, un-ostentatious style made necessary by the frequent burials and scant resources of a war zone. Australian airmen fired three volleys over the grave, the snap of their rifles joining the distant thunder of the artillery pounding the front lines. War stopped for no man, not even the Red Baron. Finally a bugler played the Last Post, and the mourners filed away, back to their battle stations.

Richthofen had left a will, written in haste some weeks before and locked up in his unit's strongbox. It contained only one sentence: "Should I fail to return, Lieutenant Reinhard (Jasta 6) shall take over the leadership of the Geschwader." Fittingly, Richthofen's only thought in considering what he left behind was to ensure that his aerial group was given a good commander. For two years, his life had been all about flying with his comrades, and in his mind that was all he was leaving to the world. In fact, the German commanders accepted the Red Baron's instruction and Reinhard, a steady flier but lacking von Richthofen's flare and imagination, took over his command. However, on June 18, Reinhard went to test out a new plane, and when its strut broke at 3,000 feet, the whole upper wing collapsed, sending him crashing to his death. He was replaced by an officer from outside the group, Hermann Goering, who was by then a fighter ace, renowned leader, and the most senior man suitable for the job. Today, of course, the world knows Goering far more for his notorious role in the next war.

Goering

   Throughout the transition process, the Red Baron's death was terrible for the morale of the men who had followed him. They had already faced increasingly harsh odds and now saw mounting casualties over the following weeks. The words of Manfred's own brother and fellow pilot Lothar von Richthofen speak to a state of deep depression: "I could find no words for this pain… a frightful apathy has come over me." Indeed, despair spread from the Flying Circus out through the German air crews all along the lines. Ernst Udet, one of von Richthofen's last recruits, was one of the few who did not seem affected, turning himself instead to continuing what the Red Baron had done. Taking over as Germany's leading air ace, in the last months of the war he became the greatest surviving fighter pilot, as suitable a tribute to his lost commander as the solemn funeral at Bertangles.

The Richthofen Geschwader, known by most as the Flying Circus, fought on under Goering until the war ended in November. Ordered to surrender their planes to the French, many deliberately landed roughly, wrecking their planes rather than see them used by the enemy. It was a final act combining obedience and defiance, entirely in keeping with the spirit of the Red Baron's hand-picked warrior elite.

Given his fame and the number of people firing upon him, it is not surprising that there were disputes over who had killed the Red Baron. The official report, based on the examination of his body by four medical officers, concluded that he had been killed by a single bullet wound, and, based on its trajectory, that it had been fired by Captain Brown. Von Richthofen's continued control of the plane after being hit was attributed to his regaining consciousness long enough to pursue May and then achieve a crash landing, in keeping with his determined character. Conversely, some brought forward evidence in favor of Popkin as the man who killed the Red Baron. However, the evidence of the doctors who examined von Richthofen's body, while cursory at best, did not match the idea that Popkin's first burst of fire caused the fatal wound and led to the apparent loss of control reported by Fraser. And Buie, who also tried to claim the kill, undermined his own argument by making claims about von Richthofen's wounds that did not match the evidence of the four examining doctors.

In a sense, it's fitting that nobody will ever know with certainty who killed the Red Baron. While he excelled in an individualized and much-glorified form of warfare, one that emphasized individual skill, he was still fighting in a war of messy engagements and anonymous fatalities.

Von Richthofen's death, like his life, embodied many of the changes the European aristocracy were undergoing. It is no coincidence that so many of the men in the German fighter planes, the men who fought in the bright heraldic colors of the Flying Circus, were descendants of the men who had fought in bright heraldic colors as Germany's medieval warrior elite. Raised to see themselves as socially and militarily superior to ordinary people, to seek out courage and adventure in which the individual could find glory, they were devastated by the social and technological changes embodied in the changing nature of warfare, changes which were vastly accelerated by the war. In a war of massive troop movements, and in which technology was more significant than any individual man, individual heroes were becoming obsolete. The life of the fighter ace gave them one last hurrah and one last moment of shining, individual glory in which men of noble breeding fought like gods high above the common soldiers.

On April 21, 1918, however, common soldiers on the ground were the ones who strafed von Richthofen with deadly anti-aircraft fire during his final fight, and it was the technically-oriented Australian reconnaissance fliers who achieved their aim in that battle and extricated themselves from danger. In that sense, it was not Captain Brown, Sergeant Popkin or Gunner Buie who got the "kill" in the final fight against the Red Baron but the industrial nature of the Allied war machine as a whole.

That fact is also reflected by the nature of Manfred von Richthofen's legacy. He had a fearsome reputation in the war, and no one can deny that shooting down 80 Allied aircraft was a staggering achievement for any individual. He achieved more victories than any other pilot, and except for the rests forced upon him by his injury in July 1917, he was in action almost constantly from the moment he joined Boelcke's Jasta 2 in September 1916. But World War I was not decided by such individual martial efforts; it was a war between vast industrial economies, and even in the air, it was the ability to put more aircraft into the skies that decided dominance in the long term. The German defensive tactics, though a choice at the start, became a necessity by the end, as they lacked the resources to successfully maintain a concerted aerial offensive such as that in support of Operation Michael.

Even within the scope of pilots' achievements, von Richthofen arrived too late to shape the German air force. Boelcke had already done that by creating the tactics and formations that von Richthofen would use to such success. Even Immelmann, whose famous maneuver became obsolete within a year, contributed more to German aerial tactics than the Red Baron. What von Richthofen did provide was leadership and an element of showmanship that kept together an air force under pressure. This is seen in the glamour of the air pilot's reputation and image, an image he contributed a great deal towards shaping. Along with burnishing that image, von Richthofen also achieved enduring fame, to the extent that he remains the most famous fighter pilot in history nearly a century after his death. He was an icon of a dying age, an expert in a bold new technology, and a man caught up in the contradictions of his time.

And like so many young men fighting during World War I, by his mid-twenties he was dead.

A 1931 picture of the Red Baron's grave in Berlin

Rickenbacker Becomes an Ace

"The excitement of automobile racing did not compare with what I knew must come with aeroplane fighting in France." – Eddie Rickenbacker

"The obviously inexperienced pilot is the game the scientific air-fighter goes after, and the majority of victories are won that way. But, on the other hand, it is the novice usually who gets the famous ace by doing at some moment the unexpected thing." – Eddie Rickenbacker

By the time America joined the war, Rickenbacker felt he could wait no longer, and he wouldn't have to. He had already had the good fortune to meet Townsend Dodd, another aspiring aviator who had served as a pilot under General John Pershing and was appointed Aviation Officer when America entered the war. Wanting qualified pilots to join him when he sailed to England, he recruited Rickenbacker to serve under him in the American Expeditionary Force in May 1917.

Dodd

Rickenbacker himself later described the following exchange: "I was at Cincinnati on the 25th of May preparing for the Memorial Day races when Maj. Lewis, who was on the staff in Washington, called me up about 8 o'clock in the evening and asked me whether I cared to go to France as one of the drivers for the staff; he said at the time, Gen. Pershing's driver. ... I said, 'I will be there in a week or 10 days,' figuring that I would have time to run the race and turn over my personal affairs to somebody capable of handling them and be in position to go in that definite period. He said, 'If you are not here tomorrow morning it is useless for you to come.' And I answered back, "I will be there,' without giving it any further thought or consideration. ...so I just disappeared. ... I went to Columbus and spent an hour with my mother and left that afternoon, and sailed the following day from New York as a sergeant, first class, in the Signal Corps..."

Rickenbacker assumed that his experience with cars and engines would make him a shoe in for the aviation corps. On one occasion, he compared race car driving to flying and how experience with the former gave him an advantage in the latter: "Long practice in driving a racing car at a hundred miles an hour or so gives first-class training in control and judging distances at high speed and helps tremendously in getting motor sense, which is rather the feel of your engine than the sound of it, a thing you get through your bones and nerves rather than simply your ears."

As it turned out, he was mistaken. Most of the men the army recruited to train as pilots had advanced college degrees, something the 7th grade dropout could not compete against. However, what he lacked in education he more than made up for in determination and practical experience, which allowed him to eventually be assigned to service and repair planes rather than fly them. This work allowed him plenty of down time during which he took advantage of his easy access to planes to practice his flying maneuvers.

There was still one problem: Rickenbacker's superiors considered him more valuable as a mechanic than they did as a pilot, and they continued to try to keep him on the ground. To get around this, Rickenbacker began training another man, who preferred safety in the hangar to danger in the skies, to replace him. The *Burlington (Iowa) Gazette* reported on November 30, 1917, "They can't make 'em too fast for Eddie Rickenbacker, American speed demon now in France with General Pershing's force's. Rick went as an automobile driver and for a time was attached to Pershing's personal staff as his driver, but this was too slow for the speed merchant and he asked to be transferred to the aviation corps where he could get some real speed. The transfer was made and Eddie entered an aviation training camp in the South of France. It took him six weeks to complete the course which usually occupies four months of training and instruction and Eddie is now a regular airman."

Rickenbacker later described the course himself: "I had about four or five hours with an instructor and then took my first solo hop, and then I averaged three or four hours a day flying alone; took my spiral tests; took my cross-country tests, and had completed all my tests at the end of 18 hours, but the rules required a man to be up 25 hours in the air before he was qualified to receive his brevet, and during that 25 hours he was supposed to make 50 landings. Well, I still had seven hours to fly, and I also had about 22 landings to make. So I started out one morning to visit the surrounding airdromes; I had an order on any of the French airdromes to supply me gasoline if I landed at them... I put in the seven hours that day, and the following day I did my landings, one after the other; that is, I would go up and circle around and land and go up again and come back and land, without stopping my motor."

The Air Corps assigned Rickenbacker to the 94th Aero Squadron, known to its men as the "Hat-in-the-Ring" Squadron. He explained in an August 1918 story for the folks back home, "Every man has a picture of a hat in a ring on his machine. That means he is ready to fight at any time, whether he wants to or not. The squadron is sometimes known as the hat-in-the,-ring squadron, but among ourselves its gimpers. We adopted the hat-in-the-ring as our emblem back in our training days. Then it was our hope to be the first fighting squadron to get to the front. Our commanding officer, who had been with the French, used to have a hat as the emblem on his machine. Someone suggested that we take the hat, put a ring around it, carrying out the idea of ex-President Roosevelt's famous statement that we were ready to fight anytime…Doug Campbell added the finishing touch to the hat-in-the-ring emblem when he got his fifth Hun, and became the first all-American trained ace. Somewhere he scared up a paint brush and painted a little black cross in the ring around the hat for each German he had brought down. They were regular German crosses, just like the ones you see on German planes before you let them have it."

The Air Corps issued Rickenbacker an unarmed Nieuport 28 to fly until they were sure he had the skills necessary to go into combat. It did not take him long to get into the thick of things and a little over 20 years later, the *Chicago Tribune* set the scene for his first kill: "It was late in the afternoon of April 29, 1918. Above was the deepening blue of the sky, below was the shell-torn earth, and a hundred feet away at Eddie's left wing tip roared his patrol mate, Capt. James Norman Hall, in a similar Nieuport. Suddenly Hall's plane banked and began to climb and spiral upward to the left. Rickenbacker followed. He didn't know what was up, but he had faith in Jimmy Hall. … A speedy German Albatross scout plane was approaching from the north."

Nieuport 28

I. Franks Valli's picture of Rickenbacker's uniform

Rickenbacker later recounted his first kill as well: "I clung as closely to Hall as I could. With his first dive I was right by his side. We had at least a thousand feet advantage over the German, and we were two to one numerically. ... At 150 yards I pressed my triggers. The tracer bullets cut a streak of living fire into the rear of the Albatross' tail. Raising the nose of my airplane slightly, I lifted the fiery streak like a stream of water from a garden hose. Gradually it settled into the pilot's seat. The swerving of the Albatross' course indicated that its rudder no longer was held by a directing hand. At 2,000 feet above the enemy's lines I pulled up my headlong dive and watched [as] the enemy...circled a little to the south and the next minute crashed onto the ground..." Hall, the man whose life he saved that day, survived the war and later wrote the famous novel *Mutiny on the Bounty.*

Rickenbacker during the war

Rickenbacker's gallantry earned him his first Distinguished Service Cross "for extraordinary heroism in action near Montsec, France, April 29, 1918. Captain Rickenbacker attacked an enemy Albatross monoplane, and after a vigorous fight in which he followed his foe into German territory, he succeeded in shooting it down near Vigneulles-les-Hatton Chatel." Another soon followed "for extraordinary heroism in action over Richecourt, France, on May 17, 1918. Captain Rickenbacker attacked three Albatross enemy planes, shooting one down in the vicinity of Richecourt, France, and forcing the others to retreat over their own lines." He earned a third just days later, when "Captain Rickenbacker attacked three Albatross monoplanes 4,000 meters over St. Mihiel, France. He drove them back into German territory, separated one from the group, and shot it down near Flirey."

Four more kills followed in quick succession, and by May 28, Rickenbacker was officially an ace. The French government recognized his accomplishment by awarding him the Croix de Guerre, and yet another Distinguished Service Cross citation, this time because "Captain Rickenbacker sighted a group of two battle planes and four monoplanes, German planes, which he at once attacked vigorously, shooting down one and dispersing the others."

His next kill came on May 30, as Major James Meissner later testified: "I was in combat with a German and just dived down to attack the German plane, and in diving down to make the attack the entering edge on my plane tore away again. … Then as I straightened out to return home, being in that condition, the German saw my predicament and he came back. I could not maneuver fast. The German was coming closer and closer, and he was shooting all the time, and then Rickenbacker came up alongside. Rickenbacker got him. Rickenbacker was a little ahead and he came down as fast as he could and assisted. That time I flew back to the field and landed all right."

Rickenbacker's Fifth Distinguished Service Cross citation praised this effort, "for extraordinary heroism in action on May 30, 1918, 4,000 meters over Jaulny, France. Captain Rickenbacker attacked a group of five enemy planes. After a violent battle, he shot down one plane and drove the others away."

This kill almost proved to Rickenbacker's last, for flying at high altitudes in below freezing temperatures caused him to develop a severe ear infection that grounded him for much of the summer. When he returned to battle in September, he shot down two German Fokker D.VIIs in as many days and was promoted to the rank of Captain.

His Sixth Distinguished Service Cross citation was "for extraordinary heroism in action in the region of Villecy, France, September 14, 1918. Captain Rickenbacker attacked four Fokker enemy planes at an altitude of 3,000 meters. After a sharp and hot action, he succeeded in shooting one down in flames and dispersing the other three."

The following day, he won his Seventh Distinguished Service Cross "for extraordinary heroism in action in the region of Bois-de-Wavrille, France, September 15, 1918. Captain Rickenbacker encountered six enemy planes, who were in the act of attacking four Spads, which were below them. Undeterred by their superior numbers, he unhesitatingly attacked them and succeeded in shooting one down in flames and completely breaking the formation of the others."

Rickenbacker was subsequently given his own squadron, and on September 24 he shot down two more German planes. The next day, he earned himself the Medal of Honor for "conspicuous gallantry and intrepidity above and beyond the call of duty in action against the enemy near Billy, France, 25 September 1918. While on a voluntary patrol over the lines, 1st Lt. Rickenbacker attacked seven enemy planes (five type Fokker, protecting two type Halberstadt). Disregarding the odds against him, he dived on them and shot down one of the Fokkers out of control. He then attacked one of the Halberstadts and sent it down also."

Rickenbacker took down another Fokker D.VII on the 27th and then spent a month targeting German observation balloons. By the end of October, he had shot down 13 Fokker D.VIIs, four other types of German planes, five observation balloons, and four reconnaissance planes for a total of 26 kills, a record that stood until World War II. He also set a record for flying 300 hours in combat missions, more the any other American pilot.

Of all his flights, however, none seems to have meant as much to him as his last of the war, when on November 11, 1918, he left his fellow aviators to their parties and flew by himself over the Western Front as German and Allied forces streamed over the former battle lines to shake hands and celebrate the end of the war.

A SPAD XIII in the colors of the 94th Aero Squadron, with this aircraft marked as Rickenbacker's aircraft

Post-War Career

"When I was racing, I had learned that you can't set stock in public adoration or your press clippings. By the time I was 26, I'd heard crowds of 100,000 scream my name, but a week later they couldn't remember who I was. You're a hero today and a bum tomorrow - hero to zero, I sometimes say." – Eddie Rickenbacker

Rickenbacker circa 1919

Rickenbacker left the Army Air Service in 1919 as a Captain and returned to the United States. By this time, he had become accustomed to a life of fame and had developed something of a taste for it. Therefore, it was not difficult for the Army to convince him to remain in service and spend his first months back home touring the country to encourage people to continue to buy Liberty Bonds. He proved to be an excellent speaker, often telling this story during his rallies: "Before going up I had pasted a poster on my machine which read; 'Buy bonds or fight.' While observing the enemy planes, which were getting closer to me I looked over the side of my plane and my eye caught sight of the Goddess of Liberty and the impressive injunction, 'Buy bonds or fight.' I knew I couldn't buy bonds just then, so I quickly decided to fight. In the struggle for air supremacy that followed two of the kaiser's men were put out of business forever and the third was forced to land behind his own lines. That was my first day's fight and the liberty poster supplied the inspiration for me to go in and get the Huns."

In gratitude for his efforts, the Army promoted Rickenbacker to Major before fully discharging him. However, because he felt that this was not a rank he earned, he continued to refer to himself as a Captain for the rest on his life.

Rickenbacker also spent the months immediately following the war writing *Fighting the Flying Circus*, an exciting account of the battles fought by American pilots in the air over Europe. Once back in America, he used his severance pay and the proceeds from his book to found the Rickenbacker Motor Company in 1920. Always in search of a better machine, he insisted that the cars the company sold feature his newly designed four-wheel brake system, the first like it in the business. In 1923, the company decided to take the company public, selling shares in the company for $11.00 each and insisting:

> "Management: The management of the Rickenbacker Motor Company is composed of pioneers in the industry, and although young in years, this company is in reality one of the oldest from the standpoint of management. The past record of success made by each and every official inspires confidence, and we believe stock in the Rickenbacker Motor Company offers safety in every way that men of proven ability and integrity can devise to safeguard your interests and their own.

> "Facts in 1922: The Rickenbacker Motor Company manufactured 5000 automobiles during 1922. A gross business of over $7,000,000 was done... In as much as this was the first year in operation, it is considered by men high in the industry, to be a record.

> "Facts Concerning 1923: During the first two days of the New York Show, the Rickenbacker Motor Company signed contracts for over 7000 cars. The remainder of their schedule, which calls for 15,000 cars, being contracted for at the close of the show. They could have contracted for approximately 3,000 additional cars, had they been in a position to produce them. This unquestionably gives a margin of safety that places the company in an enviable position."

Though it certainly seemed so in the first half of the decade, the 1920s were far from the best time to buy and sell stock in any company, and the company eventually found itself in a difficult financial position. *Automotive Industries Magazine* reported in December 1926, "Operating under a temporary and friendly receivership, the lately reorganized company is now in production on the new models. During the month of December between 300 and 400 new cars will be shipped and plans call for the production of 500 a month for 1927. According to Rickenbacker officials their dealer organization has remained intact during the reorganization period, and all dealers are now in possession of the new line of cars. The company expects to settle its $500,000 indebtedness and terminate its receivership within six months."

This proved to be overly optimistic, and Rickenbacker Motor Company went bankrupt in 1927. In spite of the fact that he was not legally responsible for the debt, Rickenbacker considered repaying those who had loaned him money a matter of personal honor and eventually paid off the entire $250,000 he owed. His car design was also justified, in that all American-made cars soon featured a four-wheeling braking system.

During the ensuing years, in September 1922, Rickenbacker surprised the world by marrying Adelaide Frost Durnat, the former wife of his one of his many racing rivals. In spite of the unusual nature of their relationship (both were in their 30s and she was five years older than he was), their union was a happy one that lasted 51 years until Rickenbacker's death in 1973. They adopted two boys together.

A contemporary newspaper article about Rickenbacker and his wife

   Though Rickenbacker was no longer in the Army, he remained tied to it by threads both pleasant and difficult, for while he was often recognized for his prowess as an aviator, he was also called upon to answer for the problems the end of the war left behind. In November 1925, he was called upon to testify in the Court Martial of General Billy Mitchell, who was charged with insubordination for his criticism of the Army's reluctance to implement a full-scale aviation program. In spite of Rickenbacker's testimony, and that of many others like him, Mitchell was found guilty. Rickenbacker was far from pleased, as the press reported: "Captain Eddie Rickenbacker, in Chicago this week for the automobile show, said, 'The trial of 'Billy' Mitchell should acquaint you with the antiquated present form of the court-martial.' The American Ace said just what this newspaper said some weeks back regarding the Mitchell fiasco when one juror broke out with, 'that's a mess of damned rot.'"

Mitchell

With his first business failure behind him, Rickenbacker decided to try again with something he was also familiar with. On September 1, 1927, he bought the Indianapolis Motor Speedway. The *Associated Press* reported, "A group of business men headed by Edward V. Rickenbacker of Detroit. America's greatest ace in the world war and formerly an automobile race driver, today purchased a large share of the stock in the Indianapolis motor speedway. Rickenbacker was named president of the organization, which in the future will be known as the Indianapolis Motor Speedway Corporation." This proved to be a better fit for both his talents and the times, and he ran it successfully until the United States entered World War II. When that war ended, Rickenbacker sold the racetrack.

Not satisfied with just owning a speedway, Rickenbacker also worked in Cadillac sales for General Motors, as well as a number of airplane manufacturers. His work in corporate America often put him at odds with President Franklin Roosevelt over his New Deal policies. In 1934, the

Associated Press told readers, "Rickenbacker May Continue 'Traitor' Speech: As senate and house committees resumed hearings on the permanent airmail bill, observers looked for possible amplification from Colonel Eddie Rickenbacker of his statement before the senate committee Saturday that the president should 'purge his official family of traitorous elements.' Rickenbacker was expected to fly here tomorrow from Detroit to address the Washington board of trade. Word that preceded him was that he might possibly finish the speech that was interrupted before the committee by Chairman McKellar. McKellar advised the war-time ace not to make a 'political speech' after Rickenbacker suggested Mr. Roosevelt should eliminate the 'traitors, few in number, I presume, who have misadvised, or advised without giving full facts, and have caused him to act contrary to American principles and American judgment.' He did not name those he suspected of being 'traitors.'"

Roosevelt responded to these and similar criticisms by Rickenbacker by prohibiting NBC Radio from broadcasting Rickenbacker's speeches. Their biggest disagreement, however, concerned the U.S. Mail, which Roosevelt had decided to have delivered by Army pilots instead of the private contractors the government had previously employed. As Virginia Van Der Veer Hamilton observed in *American Heritage Magazine* years later, "On the last day of commercial service Eddie Rickenbacker and Jack Five, vice president and chief pilot of Transcontinental and Western Airlines, flew a new Douglas transport and the final shipment of contract mail from Los Angeles to Newark in the record time of thirteen hours, four minutes, and twenty seconds. As a gesture of bravura by commercial carriers the flight was highly successful. Within hours, as already noted, a major winter storm forced the Air Corps to cancel all eastern-zone flights on the first day of its air-mail operations. This ironic sequence of events did not escape notice by the anti-administration press."

The Air Corps pilots had no experience in such efforts, and many crashes occurred. The article continued, "Anti-New Deal newspapers gave generous space to the 'air-mail fiasco.' Editorials blamed Postmaster General James A. Farley, in whose name all commercial air-mail contracts had been abruptly cancelled because of congressional charges that they had been obtained by favoritism, graft, fraud, and collusion. Aero Digest chided: 'Old Patronage Jim made a slight mistake when he started this air mail massacre.' Captain Eddie Rickenbacker, whose feat of shooting down twenty-six German planes in the World War had led to the vice-presidency of Eastern Air Transport, harshly accused the administration of 'legalized murder.'"

For all that Rickenbacker was a hero and a man of the utmost integrity, he did have something of a personal stake in the air-mail issue. Auburn University's historian explains, "After passage of the Air Mail Act of 1925, he joined Reed Chambers, his 94th Aero Squadron flying buddy, as a silent partner in Florida Airways. This venture lasted less than a year. Eddie took a job as assistant general manager for sales at General Motors in January of 1928. In June, 1929, Eddie nudged GM into the aeronautics industry with the acquisition of the Fokker Aircraft Corporation of America."

After working for General Motors for more than a decade, Rickenbacker had become vice-president of Fokker, and he used his position to convince GM to purchase North American Aviation, the parent company of Eastern Air Transport, which had a contract with the government to deliver the mail. In 1935, he managed to merge Eastern Air Transport with Florida Airways to create Eastern Air Lines, soon one of the largest commercial airlines in the world.

When he heard in April 1938 that GM was planning to sell Eastern, he convinced Alfred P. Sloan, then chairman of Eastern's board, to sell him the company for $3.5 million. There were problems, however, according to Auburn University: "At the time, just prior to the Second World War, all airlines in the United States used government subsidies to stay financially sound. The only government monies accepted into Eastern's coffers came from air mail contracts, money Eastern was willing to sacrifice in the interest of building its empire. Eddie vowed to wean Eastern off of the subsidies and did so in 1939 when he put in a sealed bid of $0 for carrying the mails across south Texas. His reward was that he secured another leg of his dream route across the U.S.'s southern tier and into Mexico."

Sloan

In addition to his work with the mail system, Rickenbacker also encouraged Eastern Air Lines to keep looking for new and better ways to build airplanes, insisting on purchasing state-of-the-art planes to join the company's ranks every time a new one came out. Not afraid to get his own hands dirty, Rickenbacker worked with Donald Douglas of Douglas Aircraft Company to design newer and better planes for the industry's needs. He also had the unique experience of visiting Rickenbacker Field, opened in 1941, and now called Dobbins Air Reserve Base.

In spite of his love for flying, Rickenbacker was known for saying, "I have never liked to use the word 'safe' in connection with either Eastern Air Lines or the entire transportation field; I prefer the word 'reliable.' He had good reason for admitting this truth, for on February 26, 1941, he was in a Douglas DC-3 that crashed in the woods near Atlanta, Georgia. Located where he was at the moment of the impact, Rickenbacker found himself pinned down and soaked with aviation fuel. Always the leader, he devoted his lucid moments to encouraging those around him to fight for survival, including those who would not live long enough to be rescued. Recalling his survival training, he was able to instruct those who were able to walk on how to go about finding help.

David Lee Russell, author of *Eastern Air Lines: A History, 1926-1991,* described Rickenbacker's predicament: "Of the survivors, Rickenbacker was in the worst shape. In the crash he was jammed into the seat arm, which fractured his left hip socket and pelvis on both sides. He had three ribs broken, two of them protruding through his skin on his side. His knee was broken, his left elbow was crushed and his skull was dented. The survivors suffered for hours in the cold since the rescue team did not reach the crash site until 6:30 A.M. just before dawn. Rickenbacker was pulled from the jagged metal between a bulkhead and a fuel tank."

Those rescuing the American hero did not hold out a lot of hope for his survival. Rickenbacker aide John Halliburton remembered, "I wouldn't have given a plugged nickel for his living another twenty-four hours. One eye was hanging out of its socket, all the way down to his cheekbone... We put Eddie on a stretcher with a defective catch... I can still remember him cussing, even though he was only semi-conscious. Some bastard of a newspaper photographer shoved a camera in his face just as we got him on the stretcher, but he never got a chance to snap a picture. Somebody from Eastern, I don't know who, damned near knocked the gut off the ridge where the plane hit."

Russell chronicled what happened next: "Rickenbacker and the other injured were taken to Atlanta's Piedmont Hospital on Capital Avenue. When an intern saw Rickenbacker, he remarked, 'He's more dead than alive. Let's take care of the live ones.' Seeing his mangled body, a Catholic priest offered to give him last rites, but he refused it. Dr. Floyd McRae, the head surgeon, arrived and started working on Rickenbacker. With his eye back in its socket, the next morning McRae made sure his patient got a milkshake laced with brandy, but Rickenbacker responded, 'I want a bottle of beer and a ham-and-egg sandwich.' McRae produced six bottles of beer, but lied to reporters that he gave Rickenbacker Coca-Cola. The Coca-Cola Company sent Rickenbacker a refrigerator filled with the soft drink."

Even though he was feeling well enough to complain, the ace pilot was far from out of danger. Russell relayed a humorous story: "Just as Rickenbacker seemed to be recovering in the first days, there was a sudden setback. The reporters told Walter Winchell, who reported on his evening radio broadcast, 'Flash! Atlanta! It is confirmed that Eddie Rickenbacker is dying and is not expected to live another hour!' Rickenbacker heard the broadcast and was so agitated he threw a water pitcher at the radio. Then he demanded to Adelaide, 'Get on the phone. Call the top men at the radio networks. Tell them to make their commentators quit talking like that. They're not helping me any by telling me I'm dead. I'm not dead, and I'm not going to die."

Eventually, the United Press reported on the aftermath of the crash: "Capt. Eddie Rickenbacker, World war flying ace, knows no reason for the crash of a big Eastern Air lines sleeper plane three weeks ago in which he was critically injured and eight persons were killed. Rickenbacker, president of the airline, told reporters his version of the accident Wednesday afternoon from his hospital bed where he lay with his left hip in a cast. 'I have thought about the crash every day and night since it happened,' he said. 'I thought about it all that beastly long night as I lay in the wreckage. I have talked about it with officials of the Civil Aeronautics Board and with executives in the company. But I have no explanation. I am sorry to say. We were just flying 1,000 feet too low.' Rickenbacker said he would be in the hospital at least another month but during the next few weeks intended to make his hospital room a sort of office where he could keep up with airplane business. EAL officials held a business meeting in his room Wednesday."

Russell concluded, "On June 25 Dr. McRae discharged Rickenbacker from Piedmont, some four months and two days after the crash. His left leg was now shorter than his right leg, and he walked with a cane. He was still in pain as he flew to LaGuardia Field, where 200 people cheered his arrival. Rickenbacker spent the rest of his summer and early fall at Candlewood Lake in Connecticut."

Ultimately, the primary cause of the crash was ruled to be the "failure of the captain in charge of the flight to exercise the proper degree of care by not checking his altimeters to determine whether both were correctly set and properly functioning before commencing his landing approach. A substantial contributing factor was the absence of an established uniform cockpit procedure on Eastern Air Lines by which both the captain and the pilot are required to make a complete check of the controls and instruments during landing operations."

One of Rickenbacker's lesser known achievements was his work on *Ace Drummond*, a popular pre-World War II era comic strip that was later made into a film series and a radio program. He also worked on *The Hall of Fame of the Air,* a comic strip featuring well-known airplanes and airmen. World War II aviation expert Stephen Sherman later wrote, "Up in my father's garage attic…we came across these cartoons he had saved for six decades --- the 'Hall of Fame of the

Air' (HFA). Every Sunday in the late 1930's, newspapers ran this cartoon feature, depicting the feats of legendary aces and early aviators. Next to each pilot, an airplane associated with him was shown. Well-known American aviation artist Clayton Knight (1891 - 1969) created HFA. ... His artwork from the Depression era and World War Two typified the iconic, heroic art of the period, used in propaganda posters. ... Beginning in 1935, the first weeks featured world-renowned aviators like Lindbergh, Earhart, and Doolittle. ... On June 23...the strip introduced a new, larger format... Aviation was big news in 1935! In the next month, Captain Eddie Rickenbacker's by-line appeared. Whether 'America's Ace of Aces' wrote the pieces or not; his name added authenticity to the strip."

World War II

"I can give you a six-word formula for success: Think things through - then follow through." – Eddie Rickenbacker

When the United States entered World War II, Rickenbacker was in his 50s, which was too old to fly combat missions, but the government had no problem finding a way to make use of his unique talents and position. Beginning in 1942, he made regular trips across the nation and the Atlantic, inspecting aviation training bases and making suggestions on how their operations might be improved. He also participated in a number of War Bond rallies, encouraging other civilians to invest both their time and money in beating the axis powers. Putting his money where his mouth was, he also assigned Eastern Air Lines planes and personnel to serve as needed.

While it would be easy to assume that by the time Rickenbacker had reached middle age, he had experienced enough adventures for one lifetime, his nearest brush with death, other than the last, was still before him. Writing in 2004 for *World War II Magazine*, Billy Rea explained, "In late 1942 Secretary of War Henry Stimson and Army Air Forces chief of staff General Henry H. 'Hap' Arnold asked the 52-year-old airline executive to travel to the Pacific theater as a $1-a-day nonmilitary observer. ... Rickenbacker was accompanied on the mission by his aide, Colonel Hans Adamson. On October 20, 1942, they climbed aboard a well-worn Boeing B-17 in Hawaii... The B-17 was crewed by Captain William Cherry Jr. of Abilene, Texas, pilot; Lieutenant James Whittaker of Burlingame, Calif., co-pilot; Lieutenant John De Angelis of Nesquehoning, Pa., navigator; Private John Bartek of Freehold, N.J., engineer; and Sergeant James Reynolds of Fort Jones, Calif., radio operator. Also along was Staff Sgt. Alexander Kaczmarczyk from Torrington, Conn., an enlisted airman who was returning to his outfit in Australia after recovering from a lengthy illness. ... They finally took off at 1:30 a.m. on October 21, bound for...Canton Island, about 1,800 miles to the southwest."

Stimson

Tragically, the men became lost and had to ditch their plane in the ocean when it ran out of fuel. "Rickenbacker stuffed a map, some official papers and his passport into his coat pockets. He also grabbed several handkerchiefs and a 60-foot line.… When the rafts were inflated and free, the pilots exited through the forward hatch and lent a hand to the passengers. Rickenbacker's escape hatch was above a wing, so he helped the others climb out once he was outside the plane. The swells were well over six feet high, making the rafts extremely difficult to handle."

Using the line he had salvaged, Rickenbacker instructed the men to tie the rafts together so that they would not drift apart. This proved to be a key to their survival.

In addition to the rope, the men had various levels of clothing, since some had remained fully dressed and others had stripped down to their underwear in anticipation of having to swim for the rafts. They also had "a first-aid kit, a Very pistol with 18 flares, two hand pumps for bailing water and pumping air into the rafts, two sheath knives, a pair of pliers, a small compass, two collapsible bailing buckets, some patching gear for each raft, pencils and Rickenbacker's map.

Reynolds had grabbed two fishing lines, but there was no bait. The pilots had also kept their pistols."

By the time the men settled into the rafts, they were exhausted from a combination of exertion and stress. Kaczmarczyk was in especially bad condition, having only recently been discharged from the hospital. But in spite of their weariness, most of the men remained awake through that first long, cold night. Writing for *American Heritage Magazine,* Thomas Fleming noted, "In their scramble to escape the sinking aircraft, no one had grabbed even a single thermos of water or emergency ration box. Then the unrelenting Pacific sun had begun, noted Rickenbacker, 'to burn into us and through us.' Several men had taken off their pants and thrown aside their coats and hats before the crash, thinking they might have to swim. Rickenbacker had watched his radioman Sgt. James W. Reynolds's body turn pink, then red, and finally begin to blister. Others were soon in a similar condition. Rickenbacker, wearing a civilian suit and a battered fedora, was relatively protected from the sun, but the salt water that sloshed into the rafts raised sores all over his body."

Rickenbacker himself recalled their plight: "There followed five days of calm. It was beastly hot. ... There was no rain until the eighth night. We saw nothing in the way of searching planes or ships. The boy in my boat had a Bible in the pocket of his jumper and on the second day out we organized prayer meetings in the morning and in the evening. Frankly and humbly we prayer for our deliverance. After the oranges were gone, there showed up terrible pangs of hunger. Then we prayed for food."

At this point, something so miraculous happened that Rickenbacker admitted, "If it wasn't for the fact that I had seven witnesses, I wouldn't dare tell this fantastic story." The famed Christian evangelist Chuck Swindoll regularly took pleasure in telling the story of what happened next: "They needed a miracle. That afternoon they had a simple devotional service and prayed for a miracle. Then they tried to nap. Eddie leaned back and pulled his military cap over his nose. Time dragged. All he could hear was the slap of the waves against the raft. Suddenly, Eddie felt something land on the top of his cap. It was a seagull! Old Ed would later describe how he sat perfectly still, planning his next move. With a flash of his hand and a squawk from the gull, he managed to grab it and wring its neck. He tore the feathers off, and he and his starving crew made a meal - a very slight meal for eight men - of it. Then they used the intestines for bait. With it, they caught fish, which gave them food and more bait ... and the cycle continued."

The men's luck continued. According to Rea, "Late that same afternoon the sky turned cloudy, the wind took on a different feel, and for the first time the prospects for rain looked promising. ... About 3 a.m. raindrops fell for a few minutes, and they spotted a squall not far away. They paddled toward it, praying they could get in its path. There was already a plan in place for such an occasion: They would catch rain on handkerchiefs, shirts and socks spread out over the rafts — Adamson even removed his shorts. The squall turned into a driving rainstorm, and all hands did what they could to collect water. Rickenbacker was designated his raft's wringer; as the clothing became soaked, he twisted the water into a bucket. After the storm subsided, the men agreed to ration the water sparingly: a half-jigger per day per man. It was the sweetest water they had ever tasted. The rain had also drenched their bodies and sores, cleansing much of the salt brine that had collected."

Ultimately, these blessings were not enough to save Kaczmarczyk. In describing this portion of the ordeal, Rickenbacker admitted, "I had been on cinder tracks and burning airplanes, but I had never been through anything like this. I was afraid to make a decision. About 6 a.m. we pulled the boats together. I examined him and finally pronounced him dead. Two of the boys were witnesses. Then we lifted him over the boat gently and his disappeared. It was one of the hardest jobs I ever had."

By this time, the drinking water they had so carefully gathered was gone, though they had only allowed each man half a jigger a day water as his ration. The men attempted to distill their urine but were unable to do so. They were also unable to catch fish, thanks in part to sharks now circling the boats. In excruciating pain due to a back injury he suffered during the crash, Adamson also seemed to be fading away. One evening, either by design or deliberately, he fell out of the raft into the water. Rickenbacker and the others helped pull him back in, and Rickenbacker made it his personal business to watch the man closely from that time on. According to Thomas Fleming, author of *Eddie Rickenbacker Lost at Sea*, "In the morning, Adamson forced a smile onto his raw lips and apologized, holding out his hand to the man who had saved him. "I don't shake hands with your kind," snapped Rickenbacker, an act that he later admitted was one of the most difficult of his life. "You've got to prove yourself first." For the rest of the day, Rickenbacker watched Adamson seething with anger, trying to decide whether to live or die. The colonel chose life, in spite of his agony - mostly because of his rage at Rickenbacker."

There was more to come, and Fleming continued, "Ignoring their growing despair, Rickenbacker insisted on daily prayer meetings. He studied each man and spoke to him in ways that would help him resist death's lure. Sometimes the words were compassionate, but often they were harsh, as they had been with Adamson. 'Rickenbacker,' one man croaked in anger, 'you're the meanest son of a bitch that ever lived!' The words only made Rickenbacker 'smile inside.' If the man could snarl at him, he had what it took to defy death. One night while Rickenbacker dozed, several of the men made a pact to stay alive until they had the pleasure of burying Captain Eddie at sea. 'I wish I'd known it at the time,' Rickenbacker said later. How glad he would have been to know that his nasty medicine was working."

The men remained hungry and dehydrated as the sun continued to beat day on them, but when they thought all was lost, their fortunes changes again. Rea wrote that "intermittent squalls the next few days brought more drinking water. Rickenbacker came up with the idea to empty the carbon dioxide stored in his Mae West life jacket and replace it with water. Taking a mouthful, he forced it through a narrow tube into the jacket compartment. Although it took quite a while, he managed to store a quart of water…The lack of food continued to be a problem. Fortune smiled again during one very dark night when a pack of sharks chased a school of mackerel through the three-raft convoy. Two of the fleeing fish landed in the rafts, were captured and promptly eaten. It was the first food in nearly a week."

In spite of these small mercies, the situation was still clearly desperate, and Rickenbacker would tell reporters of the men's last days together: "On the 17th day we saw the first sign of life. This was a little plane that went by about five miles away. We waved frantically and yelled, but he went by. It was heartbreaking. The next day two planes came out and again they missed us. The next day four came out and again passed us up. Although our boats were painted yellow and we were tied together, t was difficult to see such small objects when the breakers were in action. On the night to the 20th day we broke up under protest and every one went his own way. Capt. Cherry was alone now in the little boat. Whitaker, Deangells, and Reynolds were in another, and I was with Col. Adamson and Bartek."

What Rickenbacker did not mention is that he chose to stay with the two weakest men and care for them as long as he could. By their 21st day at sea, his two raft mates were unable to lift their heads to drink their small rations of water. Thankfully, two floatplanes came by, saw them, and soon returned with help in the form of ship that appeared just at the end of the day and picked them up. When they arrived at the nearest hospital, the trio learned that their compatriots who had left on their own had also been rescued.

According to a press story released shortly after the rescue, "Rickenbacker said that the island base to which he and his companions were taken after being rescued reminded him of stories of the South Sea Islands. … The navy sent PHY flying boats within 48 hours to pick up the survivors, and they were taken to a navy medical base at Samo. …the engineer and radio operator were too weak to be moved by plane and Col. Adamson developed complications…" In the end, all the men made it home.

Swindoll always concluded his tale of this heroic exploit by remarking, "Eddie Rickenbacker lived many years beyond that ordeal, but he never forgot the sacrifice of that first lifesaving seagull. And he never stopped saying, 'Thank You.' That's why almost every Friday night he would walk out to the end of a pier with a bucket full of shrimp, and feed the seagulls with a heart full of gratitude."

Such was the nation's adoration of Rickenbacker that there was a grassroots move to persuade him to run for president. However, he was uninterested, writing to the *Hammond Times* in February 1943, "I am indeed grateful to you for a very fine editorial entitled 'Presidential Timber.' Naturally the spirit of your editorial would warm the cockles of anybody's heart, but as for presidential timber, please believe me when I say I am not in any way, shape or form interested. I have been bitten by a lot of "bugs" in my lifetime and I am thoroughly immunized to the presidential 'bug.' All I wish for is an opportunity to help America win this war in the shortest possible time with the least amount of loss of life and cost of billions."

Good as his word, Rickenbacker wasted no time getting back to work on behalf of the war effort. As soon as he recovered, he completed the mission that taken him to the Pacific in the first place, and then started looking for something new to do. To that end, he spoke privately with Secretary of War Stimson and suggested that he go to the Soviet Union and advise them on how to repair and maintain the aircraft sent to them by the Americans to help them fight the Nazis. Because of his uneasy past with President Roosevelt, he approached the Soviet embassy about his proposal. After lengthy consideration, and encouragement from Stimson, the Soviet ambassador granted Rickenbacker permission to travel throughout the Soviet Union. Stimson himself authorized Rickenbacker to visit any "areas he may deem necessary for such purposes as he will explain..."

As the weather grew warmer and the days longer in 1943, Rickenbacker found himself flying once more along the same South Atlantic air route that he himself had founded for Eastern Air Lines just a few years earlier. General Henry "Hap" Arnold, then the commander of the United States Army Air Corps, loaned him an AAF C-54 to fly to Egypt. While in Cairo, he made careful notes of all that he saw and filed detailed reports with the Army. After Egypt, he took a C-87 on to India, where he did likewise before flying "over the Hump," that is, the eastern Himalayan Mountains, to China.

Hap Arnold

This part of the trip proved especially difficult for Rickenbacker, not because of the hardships of travel—he was well accustomed to that—but because he was so disappointed in the way the Americans were conducting the war in that part of the world. He was also disturbed by the country's political leaders, who he found to be corrupt and self-serving. Lest this seem like mid-20th century racism, Rickenbacker went out of his way to speak highly of the Chinese people themselves.

After leaving China, Rickenbacker went on to Iran, where he extended an offer through the Soviet Ambassador in Tehran to bring along an American officer. After several days of waiting, he received approval and so left Tehran en route to the Soviet capital, arriving in Moscow a few days later. His arrival came as a surprise to, among others, the United States Ambassador to the Soviet Union, who wrote the Secretary of State with a certain tone of irritation: "The distinguished flyer Captain Eddie Rickenbacker arrived in Kuibyshev on Saturday June 19 without any prior notification and reached Moscow the following morning. He is travelling in a personal military plane (C–87) accompanied by Colonel Nuckols of General Arnold's staff,

Major Sherry of General Eisenhower's staff and Dr. Dahl a private physician. Rickenbacker has informed [me] that visas and other arrangements for his entry into the Soviet Union were taken care of in Washington 6 weeks ago by himself personally through Stettinius, General Belayev and Litvinov. His instructions which were issued by Stimson do not mention travel to the Soviet Union. I understand that Litvinov had furnished him with letters of introduction to the Soviet representatives in Tehran and Chungking from whom he received every courtesy and cooperation. Apparently the Russians had complete knowledge of his movements. He was met at the airfield by representatives of the Commissariat for Defense and prior reservations had been made for his party at the National Hotel. The British also had advance notice of the visit. The first advice the Embassy received however as to his arrival was obtained from Kuibyshev late in the evening preceding the day of his arrival."

In spite of clearly not appreciating the position Rickenbacker's arrival had put him in, the Ambassador nevertheless assured the Secretary of State, "In the absence of any information or instructions from the Department I am making every effort to further the desires of Captain Rickenbacker and I have requested my Military Attaché to assist him in every way possible."

Rickenbacker's visit was far from secret, and the *Universal Press* reported on it in June 1943, "Captain Eddie Rickenbacker, famous American flier, arrived in Moscow several days ago on an undisclosed mission, it was revealed today. The Russian news agency Tass said Rickenbacker was in the Soviet capital as a 'representative of the war department.' Tass disclosed a presentation ceremony yesterday in the office of Foreign Minister V. M. Molotov when 60 American medals were awarded to Russian army and navy men." The reporter could not resist noting, "The last official mission in which Rickenbacker was reported engaged was the south Pacific inspection tour conducted for Secretary of War Henry L. Stimson in October, 1942. Rickenbacker's plane was forced down and the World War 1 ace, together with all but one member of his crew, was rescued after 21 days adrift on life boats."

While in the Soviet Union, Rickenbacker was struck by the dedication and patriotism exhibited by the ordinary Soviet citizen, in spite of the stringent wartime conditions. At the same time, he was not blind, and he also acknowledged the harsher aspects of life in a totalitarian dictatorship. He took careful note of the denial of food to those whom the state deemed unproductive to the war effort, and he later recalled the attempts by agents of the NKVD—the secret police who served as the precursors to the Soviet KGB and today's FSB—to make him drunk and pump him for secrets. Nevertheless, mindful that the Soviets were allied with the United States against Germany and were in possession of American arms, Rickenbacker fulfilled his mission and managed to befriend many Soviet air officers, with whom he shared much of his knowledge of the American aircraft given to the Soviets under the Lend-Lease program.

Rickenbacker provided assistance to the Soviets, but mindful that today's ally might be tomorrow's adversary, he tried to be observant in order to report back home what he saw. He exploited a connection in the Soviet military—as it turned out, one of the commanders of Moscow's defenses had stayed at his house in 1937—to learn about Soviet defense strategies and capabilities. He was present at the beginning of the Battle of Kursk, and he did his best to memorize a map of the front showing the distribution of the Soviet forces. He also managed to wrangle a tour of the Shturmovik aircraft factory, though this was less than successful because comments Rickenbacker made during the visit inadvertently revealed the existence of America's B-29 Superfortress program.

Leaving Moscow, Rickenbacker visited England, and while there, Prime Minister Winston Churchill, who harbored his own suspicions about the Soviets, interviewed Rickenbacker about what he saw during his visit. Once home in the United States, Rickenbacker shared his observations with the War and State Departments. Roosevelt, however, did not meet with him.

At the end of World War II, Rickenbacker continued to receive recognition for his efforts. He received the Medal for Merit, a decoration for civilians in service to the United States government, for his services during the war. His exploits in World War II were also honored in the most American way possible—a Hollywood film. 1945 saw the release of the film *Captain Eddie,* staring Fred MacMurray. The acerbic New York Times critic, Bosley Crowther, said of the movie, "'Captain Eddie' is a gasoline-buggy romance. The principal conflict in the fable is between the horse and the automobile. The World War experiences of Rickenbacker are covered in a hasty montage, and his post-war career is limited (in this film) to a blissful honeymoon. One glimpse of the hero recovering from a peace-time air-liner crash is the only vague indication of his existence between two wars. And then—back to the raft and rescue. That's the story which 'Captain Eddie' tells."

He was also immortalized in concrete. In November 1947, a four-mile long causeway linking Miami with the island of Key Biscayne was named Rickenbacker Causeway in his honor.

Later Years

"I'll fight like a wildcat until they nail the lid of my pine box down on me." – Eddie Rickenbacker

In peacetime, Rickenbacker set out to resurrect Eastern Air Lines and make it the leading commercial air carrier in the United States. Auburn University explains, "Immediately following World War II, Eddie purchased new Lockheed Constellations and Eastern was the first airline to fly them. Eastern collaborated in designing its successors, the Super-Constellation and the Electra. It also re-designed its operations to be open and responsive, and implemented a training system that prepared entry level workers to move up the corporate ladder. The "Eastern family" was very loyal to their employer. The pay-off to Eastern was that it was the most profitable airline in the country in the post-war era. Eddie resigned as president of Eastern Air Lines in 1953 to become its chairman of the board. He named his long time subordinate, Thomas

Armstrong, president. Armstrong acted as a figurehead while all the important decisions were still made by Eddie. Eddie hoped to eventually name his son William as president of Eastern, but WIlliam had no interest in joining the company."

Thanks to Rickenbacker's vision, Eastern enjoyed a postwar boom in profits, but in spite of his previous fame and success, or perhaps because of it, Rickenbacker found it difficult to cope with the changes occurring in American business and culture at the end of the 1950s. For a while, he continued to run Eastern Air Lines while living between his home in New York City and his other home in Coconut Grove, Florida. However, by the end of the decade, he was no longer able to keep up and lost his position as CEO in the fall of 1959.

Four years later, he resigned as Chairman of the Board and devoted the next decade of his life to traveling extensively, usually with Adelaide. During this time he observed that he had truly reached the height of his success because he no longer cared about "money, compliments, and publicity." Some five decades later, popular musician Todd Snider wrote a song based on the same principle bearing that four word title.

When not on the road visiting places both new and familiar, Rickenbacker traveled the nation giving speeches and attempting to inspire others with his vision for a future full of technological wonders that could change the face of the planet. As a businessman, he was often called upon to speak at corporate events, where his unique brand of heroism and humility made him a popular and effective communicator. While he remained primarily interested in aviation and automotive advances, he was also fascinated by newly emerging computer technology and the work being done as part of the space program. The latter concerned him in particular because it fed into animosity during the Cold War. Unlike most Americans of his generation, Rickenbacker retained a certain respect for the Soviet Union, primarily due to his work with its leaders during World War II. This is in no way to imply he was a Soviet sympathizer, though there were those who tried to accuse him of being one. In fact, he was conservative politically, but he maintained that the same spirit of cooperation that won World War II should still shape American-Soviet relations. In 1964, the *Somerset Daily American* reported, "Not so long ago Captain Eddie Rickenbacker used his opportunity as a Manion Forum guest to ask a most vital question. 'Are We Pledged to Protect Communism in Cuba?' ... Captain Eddie Rickenbacker happens to think the Communists are just as dangerous to U.S. interests in the western hemisphere as they are to the cause of free American labor. If the AFL-CIO has the right to speak out against the internal Communist menace as it affects the labor movement, why shouldn't Captain Eddie Rickenbacker have a similar right to air his views on anticommunist foreign policy over the Manion Forum's wave length."

When not on the road, Rickenbacker was often at his desk, writing his autobiography, a book he dedicated not to the men he had fought and died with but to those individuals who had helped him build an aviation empire: "To the Men and Women of Eastern Air Lines: It is with pleasure and pride that I inscribe to you this copy of my life story from the time I was three years of age. You will find therein the source of those principles I used to preach; and if they can help you avoid even a few of the keen disappointments and bitter heartaches that I have lived through, then I will feel well repaid for my efforts. From these principles and our labors together emerged one of our country's great airlines and further developed our great heritage of pioneering. In the years ahead young, strong hands will carry them into a future which you and I, with all our dreams, can scarcely visualize—that 'Parade of Youth' which always was and always will be the true spirit of Eastern Air Lines."

Rickenbacker continued to enjoy good health, even as Adelaide's health failed, but in 1973, the couple traveled to Switzerland in search of help for her condition, and while they were there, Rickenbacker suffered a massive stroke. The stroke made him susceptible to pneumonia, which ultimately took his life on July 23, 1973. It must have struck more than one person as ironic that, after having survived World War I and World War II, Rickenbacker still died on foreign land. His body was returned home on its final flight, and he was buried at Green Lawn Cemetery in Columbus, Ohio. Gone at the age of 82, he was the last living Medal of Honor holder from the United States Air Corps.

Naturally, death brought many posthumous honors for Rickenbacker, with the *Associated Press* reporting in 1974, "Officials at Lockbourne Air Force Base confirm the name of the installation will be changed to Rickenbacker Air Force Base May 18. Capt. Eddie V. Rickenbacker, the World War I flying ace and aviation pioneer, was born in Columbus." Rickenbacker AFB was part of the Strategic Air Command at first, but in 1980 it became the Rickenbacker Air National Guard Base. Today it is part of Rickenbacker International Airport. He also received honors for his pioneering work in motorsports, being inducted into the International Motorsports Hall of Fame in 1992, the National Sprint Car Hall of Fame also in 1992, and the Motorsports Hall of Fame of America in 1994. Cadets of the Civil Air Patrol are eligible for the Rickenbacker Award, which is the equivalent of an Air Force Technical Sergeant.

As fate would have it, that which Rickenbacker considered his greatest aviation legacy no longer survives. Eastern Air Lines, once the most profitable airline in the United States and at one time the official airline of Disneyworld, suffered financial problems through the 1970s and 1980s. One of Rickenbacker's successors was another aviation hero, astronaut Frank Borman, who became president of the airline in 1975, but a combination of high operating costs and the deregulation of the airline industry, which saw the advent of low-frills airlines, drove Eastern deeper into debt. The once great airline was sold in 1986 to investor Frank Lorenzo, who proceeded to try and save the airline by selling off underperforming operations. In 1989, Lorenzo sold the Eastern Airlines Shuttle to New York real estate developer Donald Trump, who renamed it Trump Shuttle. Such efforts were not able to stave off bankruptcy, however, and in 1991, Eastern Airlines ceased operations.

Borman

Online Resources

Other World War I titles by Charles River Editors

Other books about the Red Baron on Amazon

Other books about Rickenbacker on Amazon

Rickenbacker Bibliography

Adamson, Hans Christian, *Eddie Rickenbacker*, The Macmillan Company, New York, 1946.

Farr, Finis, *Rickenbacker's Luck – An American Life*, Houghton-Mifflin Company, Boston, 1979.

Lewis, W. David, *Eddie Rickenbacker: An American Hero in the Twentieth Century*, Johns Hopkins University Press, Baltimore, 2005.

Rickenbacker, Captain Edward V., *Fighting the Flying Circus*, Frederick A. Stokes, New York, 1919.

Rickenbacker, Captain Edward V., *Seven Came Through*, Doubleday, Doran and Company, Inc., Garden City, New York, 1943.

Rickenbacker, Edward V., *Rickenbacker: an Autobiography*, Prentice-Hall, Inc., Englewood Cliffs, NJ, 1967.

Ross, John F., *Enduring Courage: Ace Pilot Eddie Rickenbacker and the Dawn of the Age of Speed*, St. Martin's Press, 2014.

Whittaker, James C., *We Thought We Heard the Angels Sing*, E. P. Dutton, New York, 1943.

Red Baron Bibliography

Hart, Peter (2007), *Aces Falling: War Above the Trenches, 1918*.

Higham, Robin (1972), *Air Power: A Concise History*.

Johnson, Air Vice-Marshal J. E. 'Johnnie', and Lucas, Wing Commander P. B. 'Laddie' (1992), *Courage in the Skies: Great Air Battles from the Somme to Desert Storm*.

Jones, H. A. (1934), *The War in the Air: Being the Story of the Part Played in the Great War by the Royal Air Force*, volume IV.

Killen, John (1967), *The Luftwaffe: A History*.

Murray, Williamson (1999), *War in the Air 1914-45*.

Van Creveld, Martin (1991), *Technology and War, from 2000 B.C. to the Present*.

Wragg, David (2003), *Jane's Air Forces of the World: The History and Composition of the World's Air Forces*.

Free Books by Charles River Editors

We have brand new titles available for free most days of the week. To see which of our titles are currently free, click on this link.

Discounted Books by Charles River Editors

We have titles at a discount price of just 99 cents everyday. To see which of our titles are currently 99 cents, click on this link.

Made in United States
Orlando, FL
15 June 2022

18843050R00046